WORLD CRISIS AND
THE CATHOLIC

WORLD CRISIS AND
THE CATHOLIC

*Studies Published on the Occasion
of the Second World Congress
for the Lay Apostolate*

Rome

SHEED & WARD · NEW YORK

CONTENTS

Contents

Contents

Preface

VITTORINO VERONESE

This is a book by Catholics, a Catholic book; but at the same time, and for that very reason, a deeply human book.

It is a book written entirely by laymen, but its unity is the unity of a Church, of the Church of Jesus Christ, the incarnate Word, who assumed in himself all human values, giving them an eternal value; of a Church that is "Catholic", i.e., universal, supranational; of a Church which cannot remain indifferent to anything that affects man's God-given destiny, and which cannot therefore assist unmoved at the present world crisis.

The diversity of this book derives from the fact that it is written by men and women—too few women, perhaps!—who differ in race, culture, language, profession, and at times in opinion. Each one has been left complete freedom of expression, and each one speaks on his or her own responsibility and of something on which he or she is really competent to speak—and this is of no small importance, for men and women "in the news" are all too often called upon for oracular utterances on any and every subject.

But if each one writes on his or her own subject, reflecting that "temporal reality" which penetrates the warp and woof of the layman's daily existence, it is none the less true that every contribution has here a deeply religious significance and is, in a sense, an act of religion.

The statesman or politician who brings to the study of world problems not only a political sense quickened by long experience, but also a spirit deeply imbued with Christian principles; the scientist who wields the instruments of modern research to reveal in physical phenomena the trace of a divine hand; the film actress reflecting on her art with the

ix

mind of a Catholic; the trade union leader who presents an action based on the God-given principles of the natural law; the historian, the sociologist, the psychiatrist or the novelist, attentive, each in his way, to the heartbeats of a world in crisis, ready with a "diagnosis" which is in itself an act of faith and hope; the architect seeking to give, in reinforced concrete, his own response to the deepest aspirations of modern man—all are doing their job, as men and as Christians, as Catholics who "are the Church", each in the field where Providence has placed him.

In a very real way, each contribution is also an act of apostolate. In his address to the First World Congress for the Lay Apostolate, in October 1951, His Holiness Pius XII said: "It is certainly not easy to draw an exact line of demarcation showing precisely where the true apostolate of the laity begins. Must one make it embrace, for example, the education given by the mother of a family ... or else the conduct of a reputable and openly Catholic doctor whose conscience never wavers when there is a question of the natural and divine law ... or even the action of the Catholic statesman who sponsors a generous housing policy in favour of the less fortunate? Many would be inclined to answer in the negative, seeing in all these examples merely the accomplishment, very laudable in itself, but obligatory, of the duties of one's state. We know, however, the powerful and irreplaceable value, for the good of souls, of this ordinary performance of the duties of one's state by so many millions of conscientious and exemplary faithful."

The Catholics writing here are not, of course, average personalities. They are not just samples taken at random from among the millions of the faithful. Each one has been chosen, on the contrary, for his or her outstanding role in one or another sector of modern life. Their witness is, therefore, not so much an example as a sign: a response. For the world to-day is waiting for a voice which speaks with authority and for a truth to make it free; but the world does not know that this truth must be sought in a revealed and transcendent message; the message needs to be expressed in a language that is accessible, in terms of familiar problems, occupations and longings. Modern man is looking then for "witnesses"; and new media of communication make it possible for him to know—or give him at least the illusion of knowing—those who are called by the duties of their state or by exceptional talents (if it is not, at times, by the whims of fashion) to lead the way and set the standards in a particular sector of modern existence. When it is a Catholic who finds himself thus in the limelight, he knows that he bears a heavy responsibility. But once he has learned not to trust only in human resources, his responsibility becomes also a source of strength, for he knows with absolute certainty that if the world is looking to him for an answer, he has an answer to give.

His answer will not, of course, be given after the manner of the Teaching Church. The pastoral magisterium of His Holiness Pius XII also embraces all aspects of modern life, bringing the light of faith to bear upon them and building up an unprecedented body of pastoral teaching. The layman's answer will be different; he will speak from within the modern world, the world of scientific and technical progress, the world where powerful forces are welding together the unity of the human race. No doubt he will often echo the words of the Teaching Church—the magisterium of the Pope or the bishops (it is interesting to note how often papal teaching is quoted in this volume)—but he will interpret and present this teaching in his own way; by what he is, even more than by what he says, he will make the mind of the Church ever more accessible to his contemporaries.

This volume, prepared on the occasion of the Second World Congress for the Lay Apostolate, is thus essentially a collection of statements which "bear witness". In a sense the book and the Congress have had a common origin in the growth of a new awareness of the gravity of the events through which we are living. The Congress—on "The Laity in the Crisis of the Modern World"—has not, indeed, been merely a week of meetings and ceremonies in Rome. In the course of four years' preparation—through reflection, study and discussion—it has helped to create among Catholics throughout almost the whole world a common awareness of the task—of the unity and the diversity of the task—to which they are called to-day; it has helped also to create a keener, and even a painful, awareness of the distress of our modern world, of its waiting and longing for something, it knows not what—a longing the Catholic feels also in the depths of his own soul, even as he strives with all his might and all his faith to give the answer.

Many chapters, no doubt, are missing from the present volume. Some of the gaps should perhaps be a challenge to Catholics, a reminder of their duty to be "in the picture". But a choice had in any case to be made out of so many fields where Catholic men and women are active to-day, and this choice has deliberately stressed certain aspects of special significance in the present world situation.

In the first place, the very fact that it is possible to speak of "world crisis" and its challenge for the Catholic means that for the first time in history the world is beginning to feel and think of itself *as a world* ... where only the Catholic—the *Universal*—Church can satisfy man's deepest longing for unity. A series of the texts presented here reflect, therefore, and study, the process of unification taking place in the world to-day; and they are precisely the contributions of those best placed to gauge the scope of this evolution and to follow its repercussions in the depths of the human soul, in the structures of society and in the relations between peoples.

Unification does not, and must not, however, do away with the rich diversity of traditional cultures and the special genius of each race and people. On the contrary, while contacts are established and peoples become interdependent, contrasts are sharpened. Tensions are created. But tensions can be fruitful, leading to a higher synthesis. They will in fact be fruitful if they find their solution in the "only synthesis really possible", because the only one in full conformity with God's plan of love: Christianity.

To-day when relations between East and West are in the forefront of current problems, when Africa has been described as a "question-mark hooked on to the side of Europe",[1] the supranational Church, the Church of all nations, has an answer to give from the very fact of her existence; merely by looking to this universal Mother, Catholics in Europe, Asia, America, Oceania or Africa can discover at one and the same time all that they have in common and what each one brings to the common heritage.

The world which is becoming one, the world which is witnessing the upsurge of the peoples of Asia and Africa, is also, and as a condition of this progress, the world of technology, of the atomic era. The Catholic's response to world crisis will therefore be given also in terms of nuclear physics, of automation in industry, of new architectural forms and of the "technicized" art *par excellence*: the film.

Despite revolutionary change man, however, remains himself. New crisis only brings into stronger relief the everlasting and ever-new tensions of Christian living, of a life torn between earth and heaven, a sign of contradiction and of hope. And so it is on a deeply human note that the volume closes, with the reflections of the novelist and thinker; till finally we listen in prayer to the "Voice of the Church" speaking to us in the words of the poet: "Come, my children in the world, come and be my witnesses. I have blessed you, and you must be a blessing."

It remains only for me to thank wholeheartedly those who have generously responded to our invitation to contribute to this volume; to thank also all who helped in drawing up plans for the book and in carrying the project through to fulfilment. Special thanks are due to M. Jean-Pierre Dubois-Dumée, Editor of the French review, *Informations catholiques*

[1] Fr. R. Sastre, "Inquiétudes et espérance de l'Eglise en Afrique noire" (in *L'Eglise, l'occident, le monde*, Paris, Arthème Fayard, 1956).

internationales, and to Miss Rosemary Goldie, of our Secretariate.

I am proud to present our authors to their fellow-Catholics, who may learn from them a deeper understanding of the implications of their faith and a greater readiness to accept the task awaiting each one in the present world crisis.

Need I add, however, that this volume is not intended only for Catholics? Its "response" is offered also to all those, Christians or non-Christians, who look towards the Catholic Church and who have the right to expect from her sons and daughters a fraternal message and a word of hope.

WORLD CRISIS AND THE CATHOLIC

The Christian Statesman

Dr. Konrad Adenauer, Chancellor of the German Federal Republic, was born in Cologne on 5th January 1876. He studied law and economics in Freiburg, Munich and Bonn. In 1917 he was Lord Mayor of the City of Cologne. A leader of the German Central Party until 1933, he was excluded at the beginning of the Nazi régime from all public service. In 1946 he returned to public life as founder and first Chairman of the Christian Democratic Union Party. From 1948 to 1949 he was President of the Council of Europe. Since 1949 he has been Federal Chancellor.

The Christian Statesman

Chancellor Adenauer on Christian Politics and the Work of the Catholic Laity

Dr. Konrad Adenauer, Chancellor of the German Republic, gave the following interview to Dr. Karl Bringmann, the head of the Catholic News Agency in Bonn, as his contribution to the symposium World Crisis and the Catholic *on the occasion of the Second World Congress for the Lay Apostolate in Rome.*

DR. BRINGMANN: Herr Chancellor, recently you were presented with the Maria Zell Freedom Medal at the Austrian shrine and reference was made during the presentation to "the Christian statesman and great European". These words were undoubtedly and quite rightly meant as a personal reference to yourself. What is your reaction?

DR. ADENAUER: I can't altogether accept such complimentary words; nevertheless I was very pleased to receive such a recognition from Austria. The description "Christian statesman and politician" signifies a deep responsibility. We live in an age remarkable for its secularization and de-Christianization; in fact, for its active struggle against Christian principles, as we discovered under National Socialism and can still see to-day in Marxism and Communism. I consider that a Christian politician's first duty is to build up a front against this and to pursue a policy based on Western Christian thought. This kind of policy can be realized in many fields. I need not remind you that in matters of social policy there must be a continual effort to achieve social justice. There is also a similar duty to further the closest human solidarity in all matters concerning the family and in the building of new houses. In the matter of financial reform, the care of those ruined by the War, refugees and displaced persons, the settlement of grievances, and that very special

3

duty laid upon us in the face of millions of exiles, we have very vivid examples of the obligation we are under to "bear each other's burdens".

We are following the same motive in foreign policy when we do all we can to preserve the peace and achieve justice and a peaceful settlement between the nations. If you mean all this when you speak of the "Christian politician", then you have more or less my own idea of the matter.

I remember a few words Pope Pius XII said in the course of a speech to the Italian Centre for the Study of International Reconciliation on 13th October, 1955: "There are two kinds of Christian gospel—the gospel that comes through words and doctrine and the gospel that comes through deeds and living."

DR. BRINGMANN: On what grounds do you consider it right that a party like your own, and similar parties abroad, should support a policy based on Christian principles, even in the day-to-day struggle of political life?

DR. ADENAUER: In my opinion Christianity is the best compromise we can imagine between the conflicting aims felt by the individual and the community. The individual Christian has his own particular duties, such as striving to live his own moral life, loving God and helping his neighbour. But besides these, and connected with them, are other duties which can be better and more satisfactorily fulfilled by the community at large, e.g., the ordering of society, defence against demoralizing influences, and, above all, all the duties that devolve upon the State. These tasks are too great for the individual or for any society smaller than the State. The instrument for achieving political aims in the modern democratic State is the political party; so if Christians want to suffuse public life with Christian principles they must use the political party.

And then again, from the last century onwards, hostile intellectual forces have also formed their own parties based on their own particular philosophies, and are still working through these parties to-day, even in Germany. Naturally

Christians must do all they can, in the day-to-day political struggle against these forces, to respect their opponents as human beings, to keep a sense of proportion, and to act according to Christian principles.

DR. BRINGMANN: We began, Herr Chancellor, with a question about the Christian statesman and great European. Do you regard the unification of Europe which you are working for in common with the Christian, Socialist and Liberal statesmen of Europe as the aim of a Christian policy?

DR. ADENAUER: Indeed I do. I not only regard the unification of Europe as a political and economic aim worth striving for, but as a real Christian obligation. In the view of all of us who are working for it such a unification, which has already begun to take place in certain spheres, will end the centuries-old division between the Western peoples once and for all. With France—and we must thank God for it—we have reached an especially close understanding. The Federation of Europe is also the only possible basis for any general progress in economic and social matters. Finally, in the vast matter of the world-wide political cleavage with Communism it offers the only way of saving the principles of truth and freedom in the Christian West.

DR. BRINGMANN: In your opinion what part can a movement of Christian laymen play in a Christian and European policy of this kind?

DR. ADENAUER: In accordance with what I have already said, I can see a wide field of activity for the Christian lay movement—I am thinking particularly here of Germany, of course. Because of the special form of democratic government, it can operate through local government and do so with great success. But it also has a task to perform in spreading Christian principles amongst people generally and in setting a lively Christian example to others.

DR. BRINGMANN: Do you then also consider it right that in the so-called "extra-political" sphere the widest possible fields of opportunity should be kept open to religious and other sorts of free organizations, so that they can work for education and social well-being and self-government without State supervision or direction? Or should the State hold all the initiatives and exert control in these fields?

DR. ADENAUER: According to the principle of subsidiary power which I myself recognize, there is a "right of smaller groups" as against the State to pursue their tasks freely and independently in the fields you have mentioned. The State power should be thankful to be relieved and supported in this way. There are plenty of examples of this. You have only to think of places like hospitals, nursery schools, old people's homes, youth centres, welfare societies, and all the innumerable possibilities open to voluntary charitable activity. The same thing is true of adult education and especially education in local government. I can only answer your last question with the blunt reply: "The less State the better!"

DR. BRINGMANN: Within the space of a few years the West German Republic has made tremendous strides in its economy under your leadership. This progress must undoubtedly be reckoned as one of the good things which Pope Pius XII has singled out on more than one occasion as very much to be welcomed. But at the same time he has pointed out the dangers of a technicalization and materialization of the world. What, Herr Chancellor, do you regard as the most important measures to be adopted to enable the spiritual powers of the nation to keep step with its economic development, and so ensure a healthy condition from within?

DR. ADENAUER: Naturally, during the immediate post-war years Germany had to get rid of all the frightful ruin of the past. Thanks to the industry of our people, who had to make great sacrifices for the sake of millions of displaced persons, refugees, evacuees, and many other kinds of people ruined by the war, we have succeeded in turning our recovery into a great economic advance. Like you, I can see great dangers ahead if the anti-spirit of materialism should ever attack the substance of our nation and stifle its inherited virtues such as thrift, simplicity, self-discipline and energy. At the same time we were determined to do all we could to enable as

6

many classes of people as possible—capitalists, invalids, war casualties, returning prisoners of war, people who had been bombed out, refugees—to have a share in our economic progress. In this way we also hoped to preserve the spirit of mutual responsibility amongst our people. As far as we can we do our best to support every movement in the field of culture.

We are also very glad when we get help in all these endeavours from the Church and lay organizations, so as to help to develop the spirit of resistance against a purely this-worldly conception of the world, especially in our young people. I may remind you that Pope Pius XII, in a letter to President Theodor Heuss on 14th March, 1956, said: "We know what powers and capabilities, including those of a moral kind, are to be found in the German people. This has been shown again in the post-war years. May they always preserve intact and true the soul of their culture—a Christian way of thought and Christian habits of living!"

DR. BRINGMANN: In spite of this it cannot be denied that the world—and that includes Germany—is, generally speaking, in a critical condition. Fear of the atomic bomb, and a mood of despair, on the one hand, dictatorship and technocracy on the other, are all signs of this.

Where, Herr Chancellor, do you see the decisive factor in this critical condition of the world? What aims can, in your view, a genuine international solidarity hope to achieve in the face of it?

DR. ADENAUER: You are right. The general condition of the whole world, including Europe and Germany, is grave. So far the Soviet Union, with its constant threat of world revolution, has given no real sign of the possibility of any genuine *rapprochement*. She wants concessions from the free world in the matter of disarmament and bargaining policies, but is not prepared to give any in return. We must form still closer bonds with all the nations of the free world and present a solid Western front against the threat from the East. We Germans are the more seriously affected by this situation because the Iron Curtain goes right through the middle of our country and eighteen million Germans, including a great number of Catholics, have to suffer under the Communist yoke.

There is nothing the West German Republic longs for more than to unite its compatriots in the East with their brothers and sisters in the West in peace and freedom. For this too we need Western solidarity. And here to end with I should like to stress some words Pope Pius XII used in his address to the German delegation on his eightieth birthday. They have my heartfelt agreement. "We welcome everything that promises closer unity, mutual understanding, agreement and co-operation between one European nation or state and another—not with any hostile intent against others, but to make Europe strong and fit to be linked up with a world seeking genuine peace and a sound and ordered way of life."

I

SCIENCE AND TECHNOLOGY

Karl Stern was born on 8th April 1906, in Cham, Bavaria. He finished his secondary schooling in Munich in 1925 and studied medicine at the Universities of Munich, Berlin and Frankfurt. He graduated in Frankfurt in 1930, and, after interning in Internal Medicine and Neurology in Berlin, he worked from 1931 to 1932, under Professor Volhard, as resident physician at Frankfurt University Hospital. From 1932 to 1936 he was Rockefeller Fellow at the German Research Institute for Psychiatry in Munich, and from 1936 to 1939 he worked with a scholarship from the Medical Research Council at the National Hospital for Nervous Diseases, Queen Square, London. Since 1939 he has been living in Canada, working at McGill University, later as Chief of the Department of Psychiatry at the University of Ottawa, and since 1955 at the University of Montreal, where he is now Psychiatrist-in-Chief of the Institut Albert Prévost.

Member of the American Psychiatric Association and of the American Association of Neuropathologists, Dr. Stern is Canadian representative on the Board of Governors of the UNESCO Institute for Education.

A convert to Catholicism, Dr. Karl Stern is the author, in addition to many scientific publications, of an autobiography, The Pillar of Fire, *and of a book on religion and psychiatry,* The Third Revolution, *both of which have won the Christopher Award; he contributed a study on St. Thérèse of Lisieux to the anthology,* Saints for Now.

Dr. Stern and his wife, née Liselotte von Baeyer, have three children.

Group Psychology in the Atomic Era in the Light of a Christian Philosophy

KARL STERN

Perhaps at no time since that remote prehistoric event of the discovery of the use of fire has there been anything which evoked such fear and at the same time such hope in men as the discovery of atomic energy. When we hear about the destructiveness of nuclear energy the imaginative function of our mind ceases. When physicists tell us that the hydrogen bomb has the destructiveness of so many million tons of dynamite we feel the same way as when they talk to us about astronomical distances in terms of light years. Concepts of destructiveness are conjured up which become pale and abstract by the very fact of their monstrosity. This is a dangerous state of affairs. Nobody can really imagine what so many million tons of dynamite and the corresponding nuclear energy mean, not only in terms of destruction but in terms of the deformation of generations to come.

Thus far we have spoken of the potential destructive energy in matter. What about the potential destructive energy in man's soul? There is one thing about the destructiveness latent in man which makes it different from the one latent in matter—one does not need to read any text-books to have an idea of it. We all know by simple introspective experience that there are tremendous latent forces of aggressiveness, hostility and destructiveness in the depth of every one of us. In a recent study on hostility the author, a prominent American psychiatrist, states that in the United States alone overt acts of violence such as stabbing, shooting, strangling and hitting, occur at the rate of about fifteen per hour. On the average of about once per hour, a human being is shot by another human being in the United States alone. And the frequency of such occurrences in proportion to the population is about the same in all countries. Of course here we are talking only about overt acts of hatred and violence. We should add to this hostility which expresses itself only in words, in quarrels and in conscious but non-verbalized feelings. However, even that is not enough. Present-day psychiatry knows that many other phenomena are based on repressed hostility and aggressiveness. For example, in what one commonly calls nervous tension, anxiety, and many cases of depression we know that the element of backfiring hostility, of hostility which has no outlet and of which the patient is not conscious, plays a tremendous role. This goes so far that we can say quite safely that the majority of suicides are actually backfiring homicides. In other words the patient inflicts on himself a capital punishment which actually in the depth of his mind was meant for somebody else. Moreover we know that a great many psychosomatic illnesses, that is to say, true organic medical diseases, have at least a psychogenic root of repressed hostility and destructiveness. About many medical physical illnesses we can say that the person "is being eaten up", as the expression goes, by his hostility. All this must sound gloomy but it is no exaggeration to say that there exists an ocean of hostility, and if one were able to add all those elements of human destructiveness and hatred up to one single whole one would arrive at a force which is just as abysmal and cosmic and unimaginable as that of nuclear energy. In fact it has often struck me that it is perhaps no coincidence that the past fifty years which have taught us so much about the destructive forces latent in matter have also given us psychiatrists more insight than centuries before into the destructive forces latent in man. This is, historically, a peculiar phenomenon, and in some strange way may give rise to hope in us.

When I spoke of adding up, as it were, the forces of hostility in man to make up a huge total comparable to that of atomic energy I was only using a metaphor, because obviously in reality we cannot do this. However, there *is* such a thing as collective hatred, collective tension and so on, and the same laws which govern the relations between individuals seem to govern also the relations of groups of people —social groups, racial groups, economic groups and groups of nations.

Let us begin by discussing the *distrust* among groups. To make myself better understood I should like to begin with an extreme example, namely that of an insane man. Many years ago I used to have to deal in a mental hospital with a man who had a fascinating theory of his own about a certain group of people, namely the Freemasons. According to him the Freemasons were the root of all evil in the world, and in some sinister weird way they plotted for the downfall of the nations, for the big wars, for the white slave traffic and all other kinds of bad things. They also had it in for him and he could see indications of that vast plot in many signs which escaped the ordinary man, in little hints in the newspaper, on the radio, even in little gestures which people make in the street. He was able to spot Freemasons from what seemed to me harmless insignificant gestures. If I were able to demonstrate this man to-day, particularly within the setting of the mental hospital, it would not be difficult, even for a layman, to become aware of the fact that our subject was mentally sick. However, if one had met him outside the hospital by himself one might have had long conversations about all sorts of things and never have noticed that there was anything wrong with him. It was characteristic for his condition that he was able to talk about lots of other things with sound judgment and that considerable sectors of his personality seemed to be unaffected. This man suffered from a condition which plays a great role in the classical descriptive psychiatry of the nineteenth century, namely paranoia. Paranoia, in the definition of the early classical psychiatrists, is characterized by the fact that the person has one erroneous delusional idea or a set of such ideas on which he builds, completely systematically and logically, a structure of belief, or rather of the opposite of belief, namely *distrust*. Indeed, once you grant his wrong premises, his set of ideas does not seem so very bizarre and pathological. It is no coincidence that this man had as his pet group the Freemasons. Cases of paranoia (which, incidentally, are rare in the pure form) do have certain favourite persecutors, if you will allow me this paradox. First of all it is usually not a question of one villain but of a collective villain, and moreover, the poor paranoiac often chooses as it were a vast body with international ramifications such as the Freemasons, the Catholic Church or the Jews. At one time I knew an elderly lady in a mental hospital who had a very evolved system about one world enemy, namely the Catholic Church, the Vatican and the Jesuits. As is well known, in times of social landslide and great social and economic insecurity, even truly sick paranoiac patients may play leading roles, perhaps precisely because certain basic instruments of the intellect are not at all affected.

Why did I begin my argument by discussing cases which are psychiatric oddities, and of interest to the clinician? It was not only because, as we saw, pathological personalities of that kind can influence world history in times of crisis. To make myself clearer, let me make a comparison with certain phenomena in physical medicine. It is a well-known fact that in the epidemiology of certain infectious diseases it is not so much the well-developed *overt illness* (for example typhoid fever) we are worried about, but the *carriers*, that is to say people who harbour the germ in a sub-clinical way, and without realizing it are potential foci of that illness. These carriers are dispersed and hidden in the average population. Something similar is true about the condition I have just been discussing. It is not difficult to spot as mentally ill our poor man who is pursued by the Freemasons or that other, the lady patient who is so preoccupied with the Jesuits. However, similar attitudes towards other groups, national, racial, religious, etc., in the average population are very widespread in a germinal, seemingly mitigated way. It is amazing to see how widely-spread group prejudices of that kind occur, albeit without those bizarre and pathological features. In other words, besides the people who show the fully developed disease there are thousands of carriers. As everybody knows from history, in times of social unrest and economic and social landslides the resistance against that infection is lowered and group prejudices and group hatreds become overt and epidemic. In order to understand these phenomena better let us go a little into their deeper mechanism.

Most people have heard to-day about the mechanism of projection. This is a mechanism by which a person who is abnormally distrustful imbues other persons with motivations which deep down are actually his own. For example, we may encounter the case of a young girl who works in an office, and who feels that all the other people in that place are against her and that she is being disliked. On analysing her case we find out this is not only not true but the situation is actually the reverse: deep down she herself harbours a strong sense of hostility against the other people around her. However, she is not able to "handle" that sense of hostility, and the projection is a defence against it. In many political situations the same mechanism becomes rather obvious. When Hitler spoke of a sinister international plot of the Jews to achieve world domination, we were inclined to say: "Listen who is talking." This mechanism of projection can be found in all cases of group hatred, at times at very deep symbolic levels. Some years ago I read a study by an American social psychologist on the psychology of lynching, and in reading that study it became obvious that the black man who is being killed by the people because of some sexual misdemeanour represents symbolically their own instinctual drive which they are unable to handle rationally. In the language of dreams and in general symbolic expressions of our unconscious the dark man represents the shadow side, the dark side of our own selves, the dark man within; and in those eruptive, irrational manifestations of racial hatred it is evident that the crowd projects on to the evildoer something which presents an uncontrollable problem within the depth of their own unconscious.

The second aspect of this group prejudice and group hatred is something which the same observer I have just been quoting called "collective permissiveness". By that he meant that a deed of extreme cruelty which a single individual would not be able to inflict on another single individual is more easily carried out by a mob because there exists an unwritten law of permissiveness, dispersed as it were, and diluted, within the crowd.

Another element I should like to point out which enters into group prejudices and group hatred is the formation of simple, schematized figures which lack actually all the concreteness which is normally associated with the human encounter. For example, when a German under the Nazi régime of Hitler spoke of the Jew, when a man in a Catholic country speaks of the "Freemason" or a man in a Protestant country speaks of the "Roman Catholic", one will often observe that the people deal with a kind of symbolic diagram which lacks life. In order to hate collectively one has to have such a simplified schema of the enemy; one has to keep away from any personal individual encounter with him because that might humanize the relationship. Something which is closely related to this is the phenomenon of what I might call the prefabricated thought. All group hostilities and prejudices make free use of clichés. A friend of mine told me some years ago that a man from Toronto spoke to him about the question of having a subway built in Montreal. My friend wanted to explain to him the difficulties—for example, the fact that we have in Montreal a big mountain in the middle of the city. The moment he started mentioning difficulties his Toronto acquaintance interrupted him and said: "Oh! Yes, naturally I forgot you have in Montreal the Roman Catholic Church to deal with." The moment he had heard Montreal and difficulties a reflex chain of thought developed which included the Catholic Church. The idea is already precooked, like certain kinds of present-day dinners, and all you have to do is to put it into the oven.

Another element which enters here is the fact that when our feelings about something are ambivalent—that is, two-sided—human nature is such that we always concentrate on the shadow side. A non-Catholic, when talking about Catholics, evokes immediately some sinister story about the Inquisition rather than stories of sanctity. A non-Jew, in discussing the Jews, will rather talk of the "Christ-killers" than of the first followers of Our Lord, of the story of a dishonest businessman rather than of a great number of generous souls whom he has encountered.

After having discussed certain aspects of group tensions and group hostilities in the world, we may ask ourselves: What can we do about it? Many people who work in the field of social sciences believe that the problem of hostility, including group hostility, can be solved by *scientific* means. They think that we should use the marvellous discoveries of modern psychology in such a way as to eliminate hatred in the world. In an otherwise excellent book which appeared just recently on "the hostile mind", the author, a prominent psychiatrist and psychoanalyst, proposes to establish some kind of Manhattan Project with a team composed of psychiatrists, social psychologists and so on—precisely for the purpose of doing something about hatred in our world. There we must make a careful distinction. I agree that the discoveries of modern depth-psychology should be made available to educators, parents and priests, as much as possible. There is an unbelievable amount of neurotic hostility in the world, on the individual and on the collective plane, which is *avoidable*, and it is to be hoped that there will be future generations of parents and educators who know what present-day psychopathologists know about the potential *germs* of hatred and how to avoid them. But we must not succumb to that fallacy which Gabriel Marcel calls "the optimism of technique". You can produce mass hatred. The social and political engineers of all centuries have given ample proof of that. The leaders of modern dictatorial systems, particularly Soviet Russia and Nazi Germany, were well aware of those irrational forces and currents I have discussed. One uses all available means of telecommunication to engineer tension, hatred or distrust. Old enemies are discarded, and previous heroes become villains overnight, tensions are shifted, deepened or alleviated according to the exigencies of the moment. The machinery of mass communication is hooked up with the strings of collective hostility to make up a satanic keyboard on which one plays with the very soul of a people. Many of us are inclined to say: Why not use the same machinery for good? Surely, technological progress, even in the field of human communication, is not bad in itself—to think so would be Manichean. Here lies a potential fallacy. There is a difference between communication and communion. Love, unlike hatred, cannot be engineered. You can engineer likes, preferences—this is being done in the commercial field every day; you can even produce fads, certain mass enthusiasms as they come up and as you can support them once they have arisen. But you cannot engineer love scientifically. Love is intimately associated with the uniqueness and the mystery of the individual personality and the laws which govern the polarity of love and hate (although we know a lot about them) transcend the domain of our science. With the present means of mass communication people can be made to hate millions of others, but let us remember that God himself exhorts us to love our *neighbour*, *singular*. The typical deist and rationalist, let us say of the eighteenth century, believed in a love of mankind. However, Ivan Karamazov, in attacking Christianity, remarks sarcastically to his brother Aliosha, the monk, that it is easy to love mankind as an abstract but that it is impossible (as he thinks) to love one's neighbour as a concrete individual.

Here we come to one of those points at which science and wisdom, technology and humanism, have to settle a conflict. As we just remarked, with the modern means of mass communication, the press, radio and television, we can create group tensions, opinions and atmospheres, favourable and unfavourable. But it seems to me that true love comes invariably, sooner or later, to a testing point, a proving ground, deep in the heart of the single individual person. God, in the language of the Old Testament, speaks to us with a still, small voice. He needs no amplifier. It is to me no coincidence that during this past century, the century of multiplied noise, when the technical means of opinion-engineering have been so perfected, the greatest inspirations in the Church have come from hidden little souls, especially from contemplatives.

Another problem which has to be discussed in this connection is the following. It seems that the latent potentialities of destructiveness in the world to-day, together with the recent technological development of warfare, affect the moral aspect of war. It was, among others, the late Cardinal Faulhaber who urged for an entire revision of the moral theology of war. There is an obvious parallel. Just as the views of the Fathers of the Church on slavery are no longer applicable to modern times (when the entire aspect of slavery has changed), it seems that the formulations on war by the great moral theologians of the past should be reviewed in the light of the essential change of the aspect of modern war, with its "push-button" methods. The Church has always very delicately studied the moral problems concerning the destruction of human life—for example, for those who work in the medical professions. And even now there are many Christians engaged in hydrogen-bomb projects and similar activities who feel that they are facing serious moral conflicts about the indiscriminate destruction of human life and interference with the hereditary trends of future generations.

The last point which I should like to mention in this connection is one which concerns the psychology of propaganda. In view of the monstrous character of Communism many of us are inclined to point its evil out incessantly through all the most up-to-date technological means possible. Let me point out a pitfall in this. There is no doubt that we should all be aware of the dangers of evil. However, it belongs to the noblest traditions of the Church that love of the good should be greater in us than fear of the bad. The Fathers of the Church used to teach that an undue preoccupation with evil tends to make us evil. There is a strange fascination about the satanic. Moreover, this touches on the entire problem of the prophetic in religion. The prophets spoke more of the sins of the people of Israel than of those committed by the pagans. There is no record showing that Our Lord ever preached to the Jews about the atrocious materialism of Imperial Rome. Saint Paul admonished his followers to practise charity and reprimanded them about their own failings—infinitely more than he argued against the paganism outside the primitive Church. The very terror and dehumanization which goes on behind the Iron Curtain should spur us even more to seek a positive solution of the problems right in our midst—urgent problems of charity and social justice.

No group can remain psychologically integrated by a mere sense of danger from the outside. Let me return in this connection to my initial comparison. I said that the forces of hostility and fear, if added up, would parallel the force of an atom bomb. There is only one thing that is still stronger: that is love. Love does not submit to the laws of statistics. In the tradition of the Old and the New Testaments a few loving souls within the entire City of Evil suffice to save thousands from destruction. Love, as the Gospel tells us, is omnipotent. And while the cosmic forces of destructiveness are explosive and amorphous, the power of love is harmonious. It is strong enough, as Dante puts it, to move the sun and the stars.

George Meany was born in New York City on 16th August 1894. His father, Michael Meany, was president of a local plumbers union. George chose his father's trade and became a union member upon receipt of his journeyman plumber's certificate in 1915. In 1922 he was elected business agent of his local union. From 1934 to 1939 he held the office of President of the New York State Federation of Labour, and brought about more pro-labour legislation for the State than ever before in the Federation's history. This record gained nation-wide attention, and in 1939 Meany succeeded Frank Morrison as Secretary-Treasurer of the American Federation of Labour.

During World War II, Meany served as a member of the War Labour Board and on a committee consulted regularly by President Roosevelt on labour-management problems. He pioneered also in efforts to unify the world's free labour movements. In 1945 he denounced the World Federation of Trade Unions in a famous speech to the British Trades Union Congress and correctly predicted that the WFTU would become a Communist front. Later he was instrumental in bringing about the establishment of the International Confederation of Free Trade Unions. He represents the AFL-CIO on its Executive Board.

President from 1952 of the AFL, Meany was unanimously elected, in December 1955, President of the combined AFL-CIO at its first convention in New York City.

In 1919, Meany married Eugenia McMahon, who worked in a Bronx dress factory and was a member of the International Ladies' Garment Workers' Union. They have three daughters, two of whom are married.

George Meany, Spencer McCulloch wrote in the St. Louis Post-Despatch, *"is a man's man. He likes to take a highball, enjoys a game of poker. ... He works long hours, dictates rapidly, dislikes long-winded conferences. ... George Meany works in his shirtsleeves and thinks in his shirtsleeves."*

The Catholic and Present-Day Developments in the Industrial Field

GEORGE MEANY

Industrial progress has gone so far beyond men's expectations that modern men often think they must have new approaches and new ways to solve their problems. But the industrial revolution of to-day is not so very different from the industrial revolution of yesterday. The conditions which led to Pope Leo XIII's encyclical of 1891 are in some ways like conditions in industry to-day. The age of automation and atomic power seems to refer to his words "... new developments in industry, new techniques striking out on new paths, have changed the relations of employer and employee ..."— words written in the last century.

Though similar to the old ones, modern problems of industrial progress are not exactly alike. A new development of science, a new technology, is spreading across the industrial scene, reaching into places not affected by the mechanical devices of former years. The new inventions, called automation, not only replace human strength and human labour; they replace the need for human judgment in quality control and production control. We have a factory in America where automobile engine blocks are manufactured almost entirely without human labour. We have steel plants where electronic devices control the regulation of production. We have electronic machines to control railroad signalling. But the new technology has not been developed just for use in factories; it has also spread to American stores and banks and insurance companies, to our offices and our homes.

More and more and more goods can be produced by fewer and fewer and fewer men. We are faced, then, with the prospect of a wealth of abundance. We find that wonders unimagined by men of other generations can make it possible for working people to satisfy ever more of their economic needs and to have ever more leisure time.

We do not fear this power, developed by men, to help nations to grow with an almost unbelievable amount of economic expansion. We think it is a sign of the future and a realization of God's plan to have man discover ways to control the wealth of the world for the betterment of all peoples.

But while we are not afraid of it, we do not feel that we should blindly accept the idea that these wonders will automatically lead to higher and higher levels of production at lower and lower costs, or that we should think that the new abundance will automatically cause a higher and higher standard of living for the good of all. Men have not been able to invent an automatic machine for deciding fair ways to distribute products or seeing to it that everyone is helped by this greater wealth. Such machines have not been invented and will not be invented. Human beings themselves will have to make a conscious effort to safeguard progress by making it work for their betterment.

Here again, the words from the last century—"justice demands that the dignity of human personality be respected by the employer, and that men should not be used as things for gain", having "no more value than what they are worth in muscle and energy"—apply to our problems to-day. In a very real way, the "dignity of human personality" must be guarded against being looked upon as of the same order as a robot machine. We have to see to it that the value of our human labour is not decided by competition with the value of a mechanical device. If the purpose of the labour of men were ever thought to be just the same as that of the labour of a machine, the situation would be as if free men were competing with slaves. What would be even worse, these robots, these mechanical slaves, could do jobs more quickly, more efficiently, more cheaply than human slaves. To put them in competition with human beings would destroy the very purpose these inventions should serve—to work for the good of men.

Instead, this great abundance, this mastering of machines to take the place of human labour, must be used constructively for the good of everyone, or it will cause the whole economic machine of the nation to break down and make the lives of people worse instead of better. We have some very clear signs that there is a possibility of mass unemployment if automation is put into operation too quickly, without enough planning for its effects. But mass unemployment and all its evils do not have to be the result of automation. The effects can be controlled by men who honestly try to use their minds and wills for the benefit of one another.

We should remember the words of His Holiness Pope Pius XII in an address only a year ago (4th April 1956): "Productivity is not an end in itself." With this we should remember another statement a few years back about the real purpose of economic expansion, "to put in a stable manner within the reach of all members of society the material conditions required for the development of their cultural and spiritual life." (Address of 7th March 1948.) The dynamic economy of America has to be kept healthy by making it possible for workers throughout the country to buy the fruits of this enormous new productivity. Otherwise, the hasty greed of the short-sighted could cause conflict, and work against the purpose of industrial progress. Ways must also be found to help people to use this scientific progress for cultural and spiritual progress.

What can we do to make certain that these benefits will come from the new technology? We can see to it that purchasing power is raised for millions of our citizens. We can see to it that human labour is used for other jobs that need to be done—for the building of better schools, better homes, better roads, and other services that all our people need. These are jobs that will help everyone and will keep many people employed for years to come. We can develop new skills to work with and expand the new technology.

With that benefit on the material side, we can see to it that shorter working hours are scheduled to offset the substitution of automatic machinery for human labour. We can give people more freedom to spend their energy on education and cultural activities than they had before. We can see to it that the material aim is not thought of as the only end of automation; that productivity can be used to make people's whole lives much better.

In the American democracy the means are open to us. We have strong, responsible trade unions. We have the democratic processes of government to work for the interest of the whole group. We have laws in America to guard against repeating the effects of the last industrial revolution which caused Pope Leo XIII to say: "The whole process of production has been brought almost entirely under the power of a few so that a few rich, and exceedingly rich, men have laid a yoke almost of slavery on the unnumbered masses of non-owning workers."

We shall protect these means and methods and make them stronger, so that we shall not find that our liberty is destroyed by an all-powerful State, as some other people in other nations of the world have found.

We have already made much progress in making sure that benefits will come from automation. With democratic collective bargaining between unions and management, the American worker has been able to better his standard of living. As our industry produces more goods, there have to be more purchasers for those goods. We have tried to see to it that more and more workers get enough money in wages to keep the economy going. We shall have to see to it that workers continually have more money to buy the goods that are turned out in greater and greater quantities, so that the distribution will be as fair and as helpful as possible, so that mass unemployment will not be caused by a lack of markets for our production.

We have also made much progress through collective bargaining toward giving the American people more time to spend on leisure and on cultural activities. The working day has already been shortened considerably. We know that we shall have to keep on making progress toward shorter days of work. To make the effects of productivity more stable and to prevent workers from being unemployed as more and more machines are used, shorter working time will help to spread both employment and purchasing power among a greater number of people. We shall continue to try to see to it that the benefits of rising productivity are spread among as many people as possible not only for their material good but also for their cultural and spiritual betterment.

Another goal, which fits in with the needs of some industries, called the guaranteed annual wage, will help to make productivity more stable in its effects, to make sure that unemployment and all its despair do not automatically follow from shifts in production. In a few cases unions have made agreements with employers that will make sure that workers have year-round employment. This means the employers have recognized that some of the responsibility for continuing employment rests on their own methods of operating their plants and not just on the chance levels of production. It means a recognition of the fact that stable purchasing power is good for the economy and that workers are human beings who need to have the means to live all the year round—not just when material production is at its height. This is a goal in many industries where mass-production methods can displace large numbers of people on short notice, and where automation will cause more and more changes.

We have already made progress in insuring people against unemployment through setting aside money administered by the Government to make it more possible for people to live decently even when they cannot find work. As a first step toward the goal of the guaranteed annual wage, in some of our larger industries, unions have worked out with the management agreements to supplement the unemployment insurance provided through the Government. In the future, they will continue to extend this principle. More and more, industry will carry out its responsibility to workers by showing recognition that people are not like machines which can be put aside at certain times, but are human beings who should have the wherewithal to live all the year round.

Along with these advances in automation and attempts to make it work for good and not for evil, an even more remarkable discovery has come into the industrial world—atomic energy. These forces together can change the face of the entire universe and make the industrial community a vastly different place. Such possibilities have led to fear in many places. But again, we have the principles of the past, reinforced by adaptations to the present, to guide men to face this new wonder with faith and not with fear, with determination and not with cowardice. Again, we must see to it that this new advance, still in its infancy, is used to build an honourable peace in a free world where people can live better because of this new source of power. We know that atomic energy can revolutionize the industry of the whole earth, but we also know that it can be a peaceful and a beneficial revolution—not one of violence or fear. We know that it can be put to use for nations which need this kind of power to build industry and trade so that they can have expanding benefits for their people. We know that atomic power is measurable and can be controlled, but we do not expect it to control itself. It is up to human beings to face the challenge of controlling it.

This new advance is not without danger. Experiments are dangerous, and atomic energy for peaceful use is still in the experimental stage. So far, because efforts have been made to control the dangers and lessen the possibility of harm from radiation, we have had a pretty good safety record in atomic plants in America. But we are now facing a challenge of what will happen when this brand-new force, used comparatively little in industry so far, becomes a commonplace in the factories and offices and homes of America, when atomic energy as a power source becomes a common method of harnessing energy for work. We plan to meet that challenge by establishing safety codes that will work for the benefit of everyone.

How do we know how to approach this danger? Because past experience has given us an indication. We have already made tremendous progress in the field of occupational safety. We have applied a principle that will be useful once again; people are not machines. "Human dignity" is a sacred value, and goes beyond what men are "worth in muscle and energy".

There was a time in America when the profit motive was misused and injured workers were thrown on one side. Machines were repaired, but human bodies were left untreated. In the rush for profits in the first industrial revolution human health was not given enough consideration.

Pressure from trade union groups and others led to the passage of laws to counteract this effect. Through collective bargaining, still further advances were made. As a result of legislation and collective bargaining, safety codes have been established to prevent accidents and disease. Provisions have been made to help the injured workers when accident or disease has occurred. Laws have been passed to provide compensation so that injured workers can continue to live decently. In recognition that responsibility does not end there, steps have been taken to provide for rehabilitation for injured workers. We have not achieved our final goal in this field, but we have come a long way. American trade unions are still working for more beneficial laws and for fair collective bargaining agreements that will make occupational safety even more extensive.

We shall extend this principle to the dangers of atomic radiation. Everyone has a personal stake in this attempt to guard against the new hazard. In some ways we have an advantage in the dangers of this second industrial revolution, because we are starting at the beginning of its development to make sure that we can cover all the people who will be affected. In other ways, we are at a disadvantage, because the effects of this new force are not completely understood. We do not know what all the dangers are. But we are in a position to meet this challenge with determination and to guard against both the known and unknown hazards of atomic development.

One of the most important elements in helping people to harness the productivity of the first industrial revolution and safeguard men against its evils was the development of the trade union movement. Strong trade unions will remain an important force in seeing to it that the second industrial revolution works for the betterment of man.

Man's natural instinct toward association has been developed into a present-day accepted form of organizing for the benefit of the common good. Faced with the conflicts that arose when machines replaced men in the first industrial revolution, workers joined together to see to it that their wages, their conditions, and their lives in general, would be better and that human dignity would not be sacrificed to greed or profit. When Pope Leo XIII pointed out that "new techniques, new developments in industry striking out on new paths, have changed the relations of employer and employee ..." he emphasized the need for workers, who were individually defenceless in the industrial age, to join together to benefit the entire group. Since that time, in America, workers have striven to carry out that goal. In many ways, they have accomplished the purpose. To-day, through democratic negotiations, workers and employers try to work out their problems. The trade union movement has grown. Wages have gone higher. Working conditions have improved. The right to share democratically in the fruits of labour has come into being. Trade unions are a part of every-day American life. The natural right to join together has developed into a reality of organization for millions of workers.

There have been threats to this development. During the past fifty years, Communist, Fascist and military totalitarianism became a controlling force in several countries of the world. In each of these countries trade unions were crushed by the dictators. Where these dictatorships have been destroyed, trade unions have been able to rise again and work for the betterment of their members.

In America, we have fought to keep unions free from any kind of totalitarian influence. Responsible American trade unionists have recognized the need for protecting the trade union movement from being perverted by any totalitarian policy. To be effective, a trade union must be free to serve the interests of those who look to the trade union for improving their standard of life. We are free from these totalitarian influences to-day, and we shall continue to protect American trade unions against the threat of domination by any outside force. This includes freedom from dominance by the employer, by dictatorial governments, or from possible control within the movement itself by those who would try to use the movement for their own selfish ends.

In meeting these threats there is a firm foundation to-day, in the so-called second industrial revolution, that did not exist in the first. We met the challenge of the first industrial revolution by developing trade unions for the benefit of our whole country. We have kept these unions free and made them strong. We shall meet the challenge of the present-day industrial revolution with the help of the experience of the first, on a stronger basis, with more knowledge of how to work for our own good and for the good of all men.

Francesco Severi was born at Arezzo (Italy) on 13th April 1879. At twenty-five, after lecturing with outstanding success in the Universities of Parma, Ferrara and Padua, he obtained a University Chair in Mathematics. From 1921, he has been Professor of the University of Rome, lecturing in all branches of pure mathematics, and exercising for a time the functions of Rector of the University. On the invitation of various cultural bodies, he has lectured also in many countries of Europe and the Americas and in Japan.

Sixty years of unremitting labour have won for Francesco Severi world-wide renown. On the occasion of the First Prize awarded him in Königsberg for the Copernican Jubilee in 1943, Severi was proclaimed "the greatest algebrist of our day, head of the Italian School of geometry, expert master of mathematical methodology, founder of one of the best-known schools of mathematics." Many of this great master's disciples are professors in Italian and foreign universities, and students from many countries are trained in methods of research at the National Institute of Higher Mathematics of which he is Director.

A member of the Pontifical Academy of the Sciences, Francesco Severi is also President of the National Academy of the XL; he occupies the chair left vacant by Einstein in the Institut de France (Academy of Sciences), and is a member of numerous other Academies in Italy, Germany, Belgium, Rumania, Spain and Colombia, as well as of the Moscow Academy; he is Doctor and Professor honoris causa *of many universities (Madrid, Göttingen, Toronto, Buenos Aires, etc.); Editor of the* Annali di Matematica *and contributor to many foreign scientific journals; and his decorations include the Gold Medal awarded by the Italian Republic for merit in the field of culture.*

A "humanist" in the deepest sense of the term, Severi is a master of clear and elegant prose and a powerful orator.

A volunteer in the First World War, Severi was decorated for service at the front. He is a Lieutenant-Colonel of artillery.

Francesco Severi celebrated his Scientific Jubilee in April-May 1950. Representatives from fourteen countries of Europe and America took part (including mathematicians from Russia and Poland), and the Holy Father honoured the jubilarian with an autograph letter.

Science and Religion Yesterday and To-day

FRANCESCO SEVERI

The invitation to contribute to this volume prepared for the Second World Congress of the Lay Apostolate has been extended with such friendly insistence and with such authority that I have felt it my duty to respond to the appeal. Since it has not been possible, however, in the time available, to respond as I should have wished, I have thought best to return to a theme already treated (one, moreover, which is immensely vast), making use here of the most recent version of my study.

The two extremes of my article can be characterized by quoting the reflections of two scientists, representative of the nineteenth and of the twentieth centuries, and of a third, a great mathematician and thinker, who stands as a link between the two.

We are in the first half of the nineteenth century (1825). Laplace is writing in the *Essai philosophique sur les probabilités*:

> An intellect which could know at a given moment all the forces by which nature is animated and the respective situations of the elements which go to make up nature; which, moreover, was vast enough to be able to analyse these data, such an intellect would embrace in one same formula the movements of the largest bodies of the universe and those of the lightest atoms; nothing would be uncertain for such a one, and the future, with the past, would be present before his eyes.

Laplace went on to say that the evolution of the universe is attributed to final causes only through ignorance of the true causes, and that finality and free will should "completely disappear in a sound philosophy".

Determinism, Bachelard added, thus descended from

heaven to earth, and in the deserted heavens science remained the only surviving divinity.

In our day, little more than a century later, Albert
Einstein voiced, on the contrary, a very different opinion:

> The finest of all emotions is that of mystical experience. This
> is the source of all true art and of all science. Whoever has not
> experienced this emotion, whoever is not capable of dreaming
> and of being caught up in devotion, is as if he were dead. To
> know that what for us passes all understanding exists in reality,
> manifesting itself as the highest wisdom—this is the most
> radiant beauty, which our obtuse faculties can grasp only in
> rudimentary form. This certainty, this emotion, is at the heart
> of all true religious feeling.

Einstein cannot, indeed, be considered a believer in the
exact sense of the term. It is noteworthy, however, that a man
whose youthful work laid some of the foundations of contemporary neo-positivism should have acknowledged the
existence of a reality beyond our understanding—of the
supernatural in short—and that he should have ended by
professing at least a form of cosmic mysticism.

Between the two scientists stands Henri Poincaré, whose
work bears dramatic witness to the contrast between the two
historical periods and the transition from one to the other.

On the one hand, Poincaré is, indeed, the mathematician
who contributed most to the triumph of mechanicalism. His
work of 1892, *Les Méthodes nouvelles de la mécanique céleste*,
provided highly important instruments for the analysis of
problems of cosmogony and astronomy, in particular for the
problem of the stability of the solar system. These new
methods enable us, for instance, to decide as to the reciprocal positions of planets and satellites over periods of
hundreds of centuries, considerably longer than what was
possible with Laplace's elementary Newtonianism. All of
that is typical nineteenth century.

On the other hand, Poincaré presents the first passage, in
the conceptual sphere, from the physico-mathematics of the
nineteenth century to those of the twentieth, with his studies

on the dynamics of the electron and the lectures of 1901 on *"Electricité et optique"*. Here we have the prologue to the drama of twentieth-century physics, the prelude, with local time and Lorentz's *coup de pouce*, to the first form of relativity.

Poincaré's nominalism and neo-Kantianism are, however, still far removed from the thinking of the spiritualistic scientists. We remain, however, in amazement at the great Frenchman's assertion—in *La Valeur de la science* of 1905, and *Dernières pensées* of 1913—that we must be content, in science, to go after truth, without ever reaching it; that, in short, "science cannot bring us to a knowledge of the nature of things. All it can give is only a rough image. It is thus provisional and transitional."

These statements culminate in the realization that there is a moral truth, which can never be in conflict with scientific truth of any kind.

Poincaré concludes that the only objective truth (attainable by science) is the internal harmony of the world, and that the world is therefore divine, for it would not be harmonious if it were governed by chance.

All of this may be viewed as a precursor to the teaching of Pius XI, on the occasion of the renewal of the Pontifical Academy of the Sciences: Science is one of the most beautiful of all harmonies, an instrument used by God for man's elevation, and can never be in contradiction with faith.

Poincaré's words are, finally, those of the new man whose heaven gradually becomes bright once again with a higher reality than could be discerned by the short-sighted positivism of the eighteen-hundreds.

I shall now briefly sum up the process of transformation between the two extremes indicated, coming up to modern times, with the progressive turning of scientific thought towards the transcendent.

It is well known that we can trace back to the Renaissance and humanism man's rejection of the supernatural and the beginnings of pantheistic nature-worship. This trend went together with the desire to restore unity to knowledge and to return to the representative realism and the balance between reason, observation and experience which were considered to have been lost since classical antiquity.

The thinker's new attitude is summed up in the incisive words of Leonardo, the greatest of sensual nature-worshippers: "Don't bother with things which are beyond the mind of man and cannot be demonstrated by any natural example."

The prevailing interest in the world of phenomena became an all-absorbing preoccupation in the scientific Renaissance of the seventeenth century and eighteenth-century illuminism; it produced cold reasoners, mistrustful of all appearances, especially after Copernicus, Galileo, Descartes, Newton and the Kantian critique.

All of this culminated in the magnificent series of applied discoveries by which, historically speaking, the nineteenth century opened the way in the field of invention. Up till then, indeed, in thousands of years of civilization, the only instruments invented had been those operated by the muscular energy of men or animals, or, in rare cases, by the movement of water or air, or finally, but only at the dawn of the modern era, by the energy from the explosives which were then created.

At the beginning of the nineteenth century the means of communication were the same as those used by Caesar between Rome and Gaul or England, or by Trajan in the days of the Empire's widest extension.

Radical changes came about only immediately after the French Revolution. New political ideas and new ways of living created the sense of exaltation and the proud certainty of man's complete and inevitable dominion over nature expressed in the words of Laplace already quoted. Only natural phenomena and the data of experience were considered worthy of attention and of study. Any reference to the Absolute gradually became distasteful, and the sense of the divine became atrophied. Metaphysics and theology were

36

relegated to the junk heap. To glorify science came to mean the negation of dogma.

This exaltation of science can, indeed, be explained, humanly speaking—I do not say justified—in view of the miracles which, from the sixteen-hundreds on, were offered for the first time since Archimedes to mankind's astonished gaze. Just think of the tremendous material progress of the nineteenth century and the prophetic triumphs of scientific thought from the seventeenth onward.

Newton's theory of gravitation, for instance, led Halley to predict for 1759 the return of the comet which bears his name and which had appeared three times since 1531; and Clairaut had even calculated that, as actually happened, it would reach the perihelion in April 1759.

In the early nineteenth century, Le Verrier had discovered the new planet, Neptune, "at the point of his pen", in Arago's picturesque expression, i.e., by applying Lagrangian analytical mechanics to his research into the causes disturbing the orbit of the planet Uranus; subsequently, the new planet was in fact discovered in the heavens in the position and at the time indicated by Le Verrier. Maxwell had also discovered by calculation, in 1867—twenty years before Hertz produced them in his laboratory—the electromagnetic waves which were to bring about such deep changes in the life of society; Meyer and Mendelejeff had enunciated in 1869 the principle of the periodicity of the elements, and prophesied the existence of new elements; Hamilton in 1830 and MacCullagh in 1833, by a brilliant application of algebraic geometry, had deduced the conic refraction of light before it was proved by Lloyd's physical experiments; and so on.

Everything, in fact, conspired to give man the proud certainty that he was henceforth in possession of the means for penetrating all the secrets of the universe, and the illusion that nothing could any longer be attributed to supernatural interventions; the supernatural was thus reserved exclusively for the credulity of the weak-minded.

It should be added that the critical analysis of knowledge,

37

going even beyond Kant, undermined the value of Pascalian evidence as a criterion of truth. The non-Euclidean geometries came into existence, in opposition even to the Kantian *a priori*. And physical models of these geometries were constructed, making their existence a tangible reality. Nothing, indeed, could withstand the fury of renewal; not even venerable traditions of thought, reaching back for thousands of years and built on supposedly unshakeable foundations. No concession could thus be made to the principle of authority.

No one, however, in these days of euphoric enthusiasm for the Goddess Reason, so much as noticed the contradiction between the nascent relativism of the scientific theories and the blind faith professed in the truths emanating from science.

Poincaré was perhaps the first categorically to affirm the transitional nature of science.

With the creation of the non-Euclidean geometries, for the first time in the history of mathematics the problem raised by the postulate of the parallel lines, starting-point for these geometries, ceased to be a technical mathematical problem and became a purely logical problem. This was the origin of the new conceptions as to the logical structure of mathematics.

Few people at the time realized the philosophical importance of the logico-mathematical movement arising from criticism of the foundations of analysis and geometry. I have treated the subject on other occasions, and this is not the place for lengthy discussion. Leibniz hoped that the day would come when philosophers, "would settle their arguments by calculation rather than by discussion". The idea seems naïve to us, who appreciate the value of metaphysical research, but, if only as an extreme limit, it was identical with that of the first inventors of symbolic logic (among whom, allow me to recall my great master, at Turin University, Giuseppe Peano).

Summing up: Peano and the logico-mathematicians who preceded or followed him very closely led the way for Bertrand Russell, and Russell for Ludwig Wittgenstein, one of the fathers of the Vienna Circle, i.e., of neo-positivism and linguistic philosophy.

We must pause a moment to consider these doctrines, which came to birth in our own century, if only because they represent perhaps to-day the most active sector of the anti-spiritualistic trends.

Above all, there was a notable difference between nine-teenth-century positivism and twentieth-century neo-positivism. The difference lies above all in the rejection by the neo-positivists of the universal necessary truths, still brought into play by nineteenth-century positivism. For the latter, the succession of events was still governed by causality and, as was expressed in the words of Laplace, the whole universe could virtually be explained on the basis of the unchanging laws of nature, which, at some future time, man would come to know as a complete system.

The neo-positivists, on the contrary, presuppose neither necessary truths nor unchanging laws. That would still be metaphysics. Science and philosophy afford man the use of moral values, but do not in any way guarantee the absolute character of such values.

Nineteenth-century positivists rejected, or thought they rejected, metaphysics, not because metaphysics were meaning-less, but because they did not seem to admit of any empirical verification. Contemporary positivists, on the contrary, consider metaphysical statements to be nonsense and attri-bute them to logical misunderstanding of language.

According to the neo-empiricists, mathematics no longer raises the question of true or false, but is defined as a possi-bility of conventional logical constructions independent of the laws of reason; and physics, in turn, no longer attempts to describe the genesis and evolution of phenomena, but is reduced to observation and to calculation of the probable results of future observation. Physics does not know whether there is or is not an external world. The question is meaning-less. It is of no interest, either, to know what matter and energy are in their essence.

39

Classical science spoke of evidence and necessity; contemporary science speaks of convention and probability. Science is thus reduced to a system of syntactic linguistic relationships determined and governed by initial conventions; and the philosophy of knowledge becomes a mere philosophy of language.

Philosophers of language reject, moreover, classical logic and the need for some of its basic principles; they replace it with the polyvalent empirical logics, some of which seem ready-made to correct one or another disconcerting contradiction of the new physics.

I once asked a Rumanian adept of algebraic logic, Moisil, with what logic, if not with that which is common to all mortals, i.e., classical logic, the hyper-critics of the multiple logics follow the thread of their deductions. Instead of giving a direct reply, Moisil remarked that these logics have the same citizen-rights in science as the non-Euclidean geometries in relation to Euclidean geometry. The reply is not evasive, as might be thought at first sight. It makes clear that the hyper-logics have no right to pass themselves off as new logics, but only as chapters in a general abstract algebra consistent with common logic, and therefore intelligible for the brains which God has given us!

But something may be added which is more significant from our point of view. The basic objection to neo-positivism comes from its own arguments, which bring us right back into metaphysics and so contradict the very essence of the doctrine.

In the first place, a result obtained in 1932 by the Viennese logico-mathematician, Gödel, a master of neo-positivism, lays down the impossibility of demonstrating the non-contradiction of a logico-deductive system by means afforded by the system itself. And since this is the inescapable condition of all sound reasoning, after throwing the ball backwards and forwards between one system of logic and another, the last resource is intuition or experience, presupposing thus an external reality and the postulate of all postulates, that reality is not contradictory.

Another empiricist, Prof. Geymonat, ends by admitting that no language expresses anything unless its mechanism is guided by a pre-existing language, so that, as he says, it remains only for us to "accept without justification the existence of a first language or ... to have recourse to a primary extra-linguistic act which produced the first language."

In 1948, moreover, the logico-mathematician, Carruccio, formerly one of my students, reached the conclusion, on the basis of empirical logic, that in every rational thought there is an element that cannot be expressed in any system of symbolic logic, a conclusion in conformity with that expressed by St. Augustine in the *De Magistro*, that no sign by which another communicates his thought can make us understand anything without an entirely personal and active effort at understanding on our part.

But there is something more. It is a well-known fact that a number of adepts of contemporary physics are steeped in the ideas of neo-positivism, or neo-empiricism, as the physicists prefer to call it.

These physicists affirm that physics abstracts, and must abstract, from causes, and merely points out relationships between certain experimental data; moreover, that physics should only be developed from facts which can be observed through real or ideal instrumental indications. This is the principle of conceptual observability, deriving, in substance, from Einstein.

The statement that physics abstracts from causality remains, however, inacceptable; if, in view of the fatal indeterminacy of measures applied simultaneously to certain physical entities, physicists have had to be content with trying to find mass laws capable of explanation in terms of statistics and probabilities, it cannot be denied that this brings us back to the realm of causality.

As for the principle of conceptual observability, the war-cry of contemporary physics, Father Hoenen has shown that it coincides with the metaphysical principle of intelligibility. The attribute "conceptual", which no physicist has been able to discard, denotes the undoubtedly metaphysical character of this principle. Without the metaphysical imagination of an ideal experience, it would not, in fact, be possible to affirm the existence of the face of the moon which remains forever invisible to us earth-dwellers.

I have summed up in this way what, on other occasions, I have gone into at greater length on the subject of neo-positivism and of what I believe to be the metaphysical origins involuntarily hidden within its complexities. My aim was merely to demonstrate that contemporary scientific thought, even in those aspects which are furthest from the Faith, is animated by a respectful and restrained agnosticism rather than by the absolute negation of transcendency in which old-fashioned positivism took delight.

The most significant moment of the transition from the eighteen to the nineteen hundreds was marked, at the close of the nineteenth century, by the first, almost inevitable recourse to probabilistic explanation, due to Boltzmann, above all in his interpretation of the second principle of thermo-dynamics; by the discovery of radioactivity (1896), i.e., of the transmutation of matter; by the essential divergence, at the close of a century, between electromagnetism and classical dynamics, whence Lorentz's local time, the prelude to relativity; by the concept of the granular structure of energy (Planck's quantum theory), and Einstein's matter-energy equation, endorsed by the first years of the twentieth century.

This marked the collapse of the mechanistic explanations in which nineteenth-century science had delighted.

The Holy Father, in his addresses to the Pontifical Academy of the Sciences, has on various occasions studied the progress of science, adding scientific arguments to those from metaphysics and theology.

For example, in the memorable address of 22nd November 1951, he illustrated from a scientific standpoint two of St. Thomas's five proofs: the mutability of things and their evolution from a beginning to the destined end; the finality manifest in every corner of the cosmos. Modern science, the Sovereign Pontiff remarked, is nothing but one continual discovery and demonstration of the mutability of matter which had been categorically denied up to the beginning of the twentieth century.

The scientific discoveries already mentioned are sufficient proof of the necessity to reject the concept of the immutability and eternity of matter, on which certain scientists had based their denial of the possibility of Creation.

Mutability is obvious in the microcosm. Natural transmutation of matter had already been observed between radium and helium, but it was only in 1919, with Rutherford's great discovery, that the nitrogen atom was split in the first atomic bombardment by means of particles expelled from radio-active bodies, producing oxygen, hydrogen and energy. Not only, then, transmutation of matter into matter, but also of matter into energy, and so a physical realization, at least from a qualitative standpoint, of Einstein's relativity.

And after the atom, the nucleus. These are happenings of yesterday, of which it is necessary to remind no educated man. They fill us with hope at the magnificent possibilities the new discoveries open up for the civilized society of tomorrow, but at the same time with fear at the terrible dangers these same discoveries can bring in their train.

In the macrocosm also, the evolution and involution of the stars make it clearer than ever before that the universe is in a continual state of transformation from a beginning to an end. In our galactic system, which has a maximum diameter of about a hundred thousand light years, but is certainly not the largest among the galaxies, cosmic matter is partly condensed in some two hundred milliard stars; while a considerable part is still in a diffused state of very rarefied density and is constantly evolving towards its own condensation.

Ever more powerful telescopes are discovering in the Milky Way the history of millions of millenia of stellar evolution and involution: the birth and death of the stars. The average life of normal stars is counted in milliards of years. Their history begins when the hydrogen nebula, perhaps the "void and empty" matter of Genesis, at first created in a state of extreme rarefaction and almost complete absence of heat, sets in motion the formation of all the other chemical elements, in the order fixed by the Creator.

Globally speaking, however, despite the alternation of life and death, the universe is growing old with the increase of total entropy. Energy tends to decrease in strength, to degenerate into less and less utilizable forms. Everything is tending towards homogeneity, towards absolute uniformity, and once this is reached, the visible universe will be no more, and another heaven will not be able to come into being without a new divine intervention.

Finality appears also more clearly than ever in the great mystery of organic life and of our rational life. There is no explanation for intuition and abstraction, self-consciousness and self-determination, which are the essence of our spiritual nature.

The observable fact that the rational soul, unlike the sensitive soul, is not localized in any part of the human body, corresponds fully to the conclusion reached to-day by the majority of biologists, and physicists, chemists and mathematicians concerned with biology: that vital finality cannot be convincingly explained on any materialistic grounds.

Schrödinger, one of the creators of wave mechanics, in his well-known work, *What is Life?*, points out that statistical laws, successfully used in nuclear physics where the laws of probability can be applied to large numbers, are inadequate for the large proteinic molecules composed of a relatively small number of atoms; and he does not hesitate to speak of vital phenomena with negative entropy. These are phenomena of synthesis, bringing order out of disorder, the heterogeneous out of the homogeneous; more probable states out of less probable states; producing new inequalities of energy, contrary to the second principle of thermodynamics;

contrary, in short, to the whole complex of physical facts which lead organic and inorganic life towards death.

The origin of life, naturalistically speaking, is a mystery, as all serious scientists admit. The serious scientist, if he is not a believer, must at least have the honesty to repeat with Socrates: "I know that I do not know". Lecomte de Noüy, dealing with these problems from the physico-mathematical point of view, demonstrated the tremendous improbability of the formation of vital substances, which, however, in actual fact, are formed. The probability of the formation of a protein is one favourable chance to an immense number of unfavourable chances, expressed by 1 followed by 1360 zeros.

This same scientific genius, returning to the faith after thirty years of atheism, wrote: "Those who, without any proof, have systematically endeavoured to destroy the idea of God, have done something anti-scientific."

Man, in short, ends by rediscovering everywhere, in the immensity of the universe, in the infinite littleness of the atom, and finally within himself, in the rise, the flux and the cessation of life, the adorable sign of God's presence.

I shall mention briefly another aspect of our survey which may not be overlooked: the absolute and the relative.

I once gave a talk entitled "The Absolutes of Relativity". I cannot enumerate these absolutes here. I shall only say, by way of synthesis, that the theory of relativity is the most refined quest for the absolute. It proposes, in fact, to discover laws which are equally perceptible to all thinking and observing subjects. In technical language, these are the invariant laws, i.e., laws independent of the system of reference. The theory further states the relativity of certain measures (e.g., of time, while leaving naturally intact the psychological notion of time), as a warning against their fallacy and in an attempt to discover measurements of physical entities which will appear identical for every observer.

The progress of the theory, due both to Einstein and to a

brilliant galaxy of research-workers throughout the world, has brought us from the early relativity of 1905, a mere mathematical abstraction of a four-dimensional space-time, void of matter and energy, to the latest theory enunciated by Einstein in 1953, passing through the successive stages reached in 1916 and 1950. Gradually the picture has been completed with the phenomena of the macrocosm, whether gravitational or electro-magnetic, and finally those of the microcosm.

The complex of physical facts brought together by this theory appears finally (in conformity with the intuition of Riemann and Clifford in the nineteenth century) as a series of properties linked only by the geometrical structure of space and independent of the system of co-ordinates chosen.

The latest unitary theory reinstates the continuity of energy and unreservedly rejects quantification, which had been affirmed also by Einstein himself. With the quanta and the wave mechanics of Schrödinger and De Broglie, the universe had been obscured by the corpuscle-wave dualism, by indeterminacy and the consequent suppression of causality. Speaking of the probabilistic attitude resulting from this situation, Einstein once exclaimed: "I cannot believe that God is playing dice with the universe." The remark does not, however, seem to me justified, for, if we can perceive certain aspects of truth only as probabilities, we cannot deduce from this that the absolute laws by which God governs the world and of which only pale reflections are known to us, must also be mere probabilities!

Einstein considered that for the present an insurmountable barrier stood between his latest theory and experimental verification. I go a little further. It seems to me that such verification is prevented by the fact that, whereas the theory henceforth inserts all phenomena in space-time, space must inevitably be separated from time in experimentation. It is, in short, our human lot to be unable to penetrate beyond certain limits into what for us is mystery.

Nineteenth-century science believed that man would one

day find the key to the universe. Science to-day knows, on the contrary, that man can only proceed towards truth by an endless series of approximations. If, indeed, man came to possess the key to the universe, he would become God, able to create and to annihilate; and no one in his senses can think such a thing!

We come thus to the last subject of this article: machines. There are very many people to-day who find in the wonderful progress of machinery new arguments in favour of the notion of man as a creator who does not need God.

A new branch of science recently came into being, due essentially to Norbert Wiener, a volcanic intellect of world-wide fame, from the Massachusetts Institute of Technology: cybernetics (from the Greek word meaning "steersman"). Deriving from the technique of electrical communication and the behaviour of electronic calculators, this science studies the controls communicated from man to man, from man to machine and from machine to machine. Machines, indeed, are also, like men, communicating organisms and have a certain capacity of auto-control or self-adjustment when faced with unforeseen and dangerous circumstances.

Automatic machines have reached such a state of perfection and competence that some are styled "brains". One of Wiener's colleagues, Shannon, has constructed an automatic machine which plays chess.

Here, however, we must part company immediately and clearly with metaphors which present a danger for the uninitiated public, who hear these things repeated, at times with anti-religious intent, and believe in what does not in reality exist. The terms used here are only an analogical language, justified by its power of suggestion and by certain resemblances, which, however, do not touch the depths of life and the spirit.

Electronic "brains" are not brains; mechanical players are not players endowed with absolute freedom of initiative either in the right or the wrong direction, but mere automata; they do what we have previously willed them to do, with a will we cannot afterwards change without destroying the wonderful machine.

I read recently a newspaper interview with Enrico Fermi by an impartial witness. According to Fermi, the giant electronic brain in Madison Avenue, New York, makes mistakes, has its moods and works better in the evening than in the morning. And yet, the great physicist continues, there is neither magic nor miracle in this; the machine simply does what man has taught it to do; stupidly even, for it only knows how to add and to subtract; but it does the additions and subtractions infinitely quicker than the human brain.

So says Fermi. The miracle, then, is only in the rapidity of the operations effected. But do we call the aeroplane miraculous because it is so much quicker than a man on foot? It is man who has so conceived and constructed it. The humblest mathematician knows, moreover, that the invention of methods of numerical calculation is a mathematical creation, while the application of the methods is an affair for machines or clerks.

Wiener himself, moreover, with attractive sincerity, goes so far as to admit his own innocent "narcissism" and to exclaim: "The inventors of wonderful new machines are perhaps only trying to flabbergast people."

We must not let ourselves be flabbergasted, however, to the point of forgetting that no machine has unlimited freedom of choice—free will, in short. A self-regulator, like the speed-regulator on a motor for instance, when receiving a sudden stimulus, must react in a given way; a human being, on the contrary, on receiving a stimulus, can even fail to react, or can react in one way rather than another.

What, however, require serious consideration are the human and social effects of machines in the "onrush" of modern science.

Many years back, the Japanese writer, Anesaki, pointed out that man must master the machine if he is not to become its slave; and the poet, Giuseppe Ungaretti, wrote not long ago: "There is a force, the force of the machine, which leaves us ever more defenceless before its blindness. ... What can man do in order not to be dehumanized by the machine, to master it, to make it morally an instrument of progress? ... How can man feel his greatness in face of the machine, deriving strength only from his weak flesh? Moral strength!" Here lies the whole problem.

Wiener echoes the poets, and, even if he is more or less an agnostic as far as religion is concerned, he is a convinced supporter of moral values. Man, he says, must "know what he wants". He must know the machine well in order to master it. Moreover, he continues, "the existence of the soul, whatever is meant by this term, is not accessible to the scientific methods of cybernetics." And elsewhere: "Mechanization ... is tending to do away with mankind's moral values."

His forecasts for the future are therefore terribly gloomy ones. "Fear generates an Apocalyptic spiral: each new and terrifying discovery only increases the need for a further discovery ... the use of the new weapons will increase the entropy of our planet, until all distinctions between good and evil, man and matter disappear in the white furnace of a new star. We have drawn down upon ourselves the demons of our day ... and our nervous obsession with the harnessing of scientific discovery is dragging us into the abyss of self-destruction."

Elsewhere, Wiener affirms, less pessimistically, that another war would bring about in less than five years the full development of the age of automation. The result would be disastrous confusion and terrible unemployment.

"Our grandfathers" Wiener goes on to say "tasted the fruit of the tree of science and to-day this fruit also has a bitter taste in our mouths; the Angel with the flaming sword stands henceforth above us. ... Time is short, and the hour is now imminent when we must choose between good and evil."

Thinking men, before it is too late, heed and meditate on

these words of an agnostic. Let those who are still far away, return to God; and let him who has the greatest moral responsibility seek to break through the barriers of hatred set between peoples, spreading that true Christian civilization in which the claims of the spirit are harmonized with material wellbeing, with social justice and with respect for freedom and the human personality.

Juan José Lopez-Ibor studied medicine in Valencia. After an internship in Forensic Medicine, he specialized in psychiatry and took his doctorate in Madrid in 1930, doing further post-graduate study in Zürich, Paris and in various German institutes. His first professional post was at the Mental Hospital in Valencia, where he was later Director. He is now in Madrid, as Director of the Neuro-Psychiatric Clinic of the Provincial Hospital and Professor of Medical Psychology in the Faculty of Medicine.

Dr. Lopez-Ibor is widely known outside his own country, having lectured at various international congresses on psychiatry and also at the invitation of Governments (Venuezuela and Brazil) and scientific institutes (in Sweden, Austria, Switzerland, etc.). Professor honoris causa *at St. Mark's University in Lima, he is a member of many scientific societies both in Europe and in the Americas. He was Chairman of the International Congress of Neurology and Psychiatry, and is delegate in Spain of the International Academy of Legal Medicine and Social Medicine. At the Congress in Ettal (Germany), he was made President of the Catholic International Society for Clinical Psychology and Psycho-Therapy.*

Editor of the quarterly review, Actas Luso-Españolas de Neurologia y Psiquiatria, *Dr. Lopez-Ibor is author, among other works, of:* La agonía del Psicoanálisis (*Espasa Calpe, Austral.*), La Angustia Vital (*Paz Montalvo, 1950*), Los problemas de la enfermedades mentales (*Labor, 1949*), Epilepsia genuina (*Morata, 1942*), Neurosis de Guerra (*Barcelona, Ed. Cientifico-Médica, 1941*), Lo vivo y lo muerto del psicoanálisis (*Barcelona, Miracle, 1935*), Descubrimiento de la intimidad (*Labor, 1953*) *and* El Español y su complejo de inferioridad.

Catholics and the Current Evolution of Medicine

JUAN JOSÉ LOPEZ-IBOR

The changes that are taking place in modern medicine are crystallizing in three directions:

In the first place, medicine is following the line of *technical progress* to a truly wonderful degree. The average age of man has increased by more than a decade, infantile mortality has decreased considerably and, in the struggle against infectious diseases, victories have been won that could scarcely have been imagined twenty years ago. Undoubted progress has been made in diagnostic techniques in the battle against diseases still as enigmatic as cancer. In fact, diagnostic and therapeutic techniques are advancing more rapidly than the scientific understanding of disease. There are diseases full of etiological and pathogenic obscurities which, nevertheless, the doctor knows how to treat, and does treat, therapeutically. Technique, which seems own daughter of progress in the natural-scientific understanding of disease, is becoming independent and is acting on its own. (This is creating certain moral problems to which I shall refer later.) The benefits of modern medical technical methods are most evident in the human group which lives within the orbit of what we are accustomed to call western civilization.

In the second place, medicine has allowed itself to be infiltrated by the *social spirit of the age*. This is a complex phenomenon. Increasing progress in industrialization makes it natural that society should demand a guarantee of medical assistance for those who injure themselves or fall ill in the course of their work. From this the next step was to the principle of guaranteed medical aid for the greatest possible number of inhabitants of a country. Technical progress in medicine has led of itself to a rise in the cost of medical aid.

The diagnostic and therapeutic methods employed by present-day doctors are much more expensive than those which were in use at the beginning of the century, and as a result, the demand for the socialization of medicine is implicit in the dialectics of technical progress.

Such a situation, however, is not free of paradox. While it is certain that progress has been made in therapeutic methods, it is equally certain that there is everywhere a growing need to increase the number of hospital beds and that, in general, the number of chronic sick has also increased. Many diseases which formerly offered a high coefficient of mortality no longer exercise this exterminatory power but contribute instead to populating the world with invalids.

Disease always manifests itself in two ways in a sick person: objectively, as a biological disturbance, and *subjectively*, as a suffering. In acute diseases, in those which develop rapidly, the pathic stream ("disease as suffering") is less evident than in those which take longer to develop and which become chronic. Moreover, medical theoreticians have not yet been able to formulate a definition of a disease in which the only things they know for certain are the objective disorders which express it. The difficulty always lies in determining the frontier between the healthy and the sick person. This boundary is a fluid front which shows numerous variations. Experience shows that the setting up of social insurance is increasing the number of those who register themselves as sick. There is no objective rule for deciding this simple question; for that reason clinical medicine preserves its supremacy and will never be absorbed in technical progress. Clinical medicine is a matter of learning, rather than pure knowledge.

Along with the growing emphasis on the technical side of medicine, and its socialization, there has appeared the third trend which characterizes present-day medicine: psychology. It is often believed that the current interest in psychological questions in the field of disease proceeds from the increase in the number of persons who become mentally ill as a result of modern life. The facts are not so simple. There exists a group of mentally ill persons which, like that of other organically sick people, remains relatively immune, as regards frequency of incidence, to the fluctuations of the social structure. On the other hand, there also exists a large group of such persons which does reflect these variations. The importance of psychological problems in illness is apparent in every case of physical sickness. The subjective symptoms, and the way in which they are suffered, have to be included in everything relating to diagnosis and therapeutic treatment.

Moreover, the two preceding processes, technicization and socialization, disturb the doctor-patient relationship, which is always a personal rather than a merely individual relationship, and which is necessary to the therapeutic process. From this it results that, alongside this tremendous progress in modern medicine, so many forms of charlatanism persist so obstinately. The sick person needs to be cared for in his distress and to be understood in his pain and suffering. The influence of personal and social factors in the determination and course of many diseases is clear. There are not only physical but also psychological traumas, and a new trend in present-day medicine is dealing with this angle. Psychosomatic medicine is not one more specialist branch but rather a serious endeavour to consider the problem of the sick person from a more complete perspective. It is a mistake to believe that psychological factors only operate in those illnesses which are called psychic or mental: man is a unit, both when he is well and when he is ill. In the clearest case of organic disease we still have to take these psychological aspects into account.

This threefold change in medicine arises from a deeper level. In short, it all comes down to the recognition of a basic truth: that human nature is something more than pure biology or pure physio-chemistry. In fine, the great advance of modern medicine consists in this rediscovery of the personal roots of disease. Sickness is not a purely physical, chemical or even biological event, but a personal one. A gastric ulcer in a dog is not the same as an ulcer in a man, in spite of all the points of resemblance.

From this we come to what the Church has had to make clear so often, in recent times, with respect to medical problems. It is necessary, in regard to technical methods, to define their limits. No mere experimenting on man whatever is permissible; no therapeutic treatment may be simply tested out on him. The limits are not set by the technical principles themselves, but derive rather from the consideration of man as a person. And how often these limits have been over-stepped! Even to-day there is a great deal of confusion over this point. In no case may the doctor dispose of a human life, nor may he elect to sacrifice it for another. The greater the power of technique, the more prudence is necessary in its employment. Precisely because he has a greater effectiveness, the modern doctor needs to have all the more ready a grasp of his moral principles. The triumphs of medicine have increased confidence in doctors, and that change is evident in psychological medicine. Nowadays the doctor, and especially the psychiatrist, is consulted on problems that were formerly taken to the confessor. This is a consequence of the secularization of modern society. Such a procedure does not constitute anything evil in itself—but only when the doctor does not possess the necessary personal "formation" to deal with such problems. Undoubtedly there exists a series of psychopathological techniques and a mass of psychological learning, which help in the task and which, above all, make it possible to isolate what there is of the diseased or anomalous in conduct that is apparently normal; but technique is not enough unless it rests on a clear distinction of the hierarchy of human values from the technique which is applied.

For the present-day doctor, the moral code drawn up on Hippocratic principles is inadequate, in spite of its historical greatness. The doctor of to-day knows more of the life of his patient; much more than the doctor of other epochs. The obligation of professional secrecy is greater. For that reason the Supreme Pontiff has repeatedly called attention to medico-moral problems.

The doctor must respect the patient. Scientific knowledge always carries with it a source of aggressivity, and when the reality that has to be explored is human disease, aggressivity has to be compensated for by respect. There is no true medicine which is not based on a consideration of man as the repository of spiritual values. The Church keeps a continual watch and warns against the dangers of transgressing the limits of that view.

If the true make-up of a human being is forgotten, disease is a pure absurdity, as too is pain. It is not, then, surprising that it should have been maintained, for example, that birth-pangs are something superimposed on the biological order itself, as a kind of conditioned reflex. A purely rational concept of man leads of necessity to his dehumanization. Pain and suffering are not ruled by any logical process and pain is neither a conditioned reflex nor a defensive reflex. There are grave illnesses which pursue their course surreptitiously, without any symptoms revealing them until they are in their last stages. There are slight illnesses which are accompanied by painful symptoms out of all proportion to the danger of the disease. There are illnesses which consist purely in pain, and others which are pure suffering. Thus to seek to explain the presence of pain simply as a defensive reaction is not only inadequate, but also erroneous; it is an error deriving from certain scientific views which are on the point of being superceded. To seek to explain human conduct as the result of conditioned reflexes is to persist in ignoring the human factor in conduct. To hold that man's psychological dynamics consist in purely instinctive dynamics, as some schools of psychology claim, is to be content with a very poor interpretation of man. The erroneousness of such claims is made clear by daily clinical experience, and it is precisely this that is forcing modern medical thought into new channels.

Pain and suffering cannot have *a meaning* that is to be found *within* human life itself. One great danger of the

57

growth of the psychological evaluation of disease lies precisely in this introduction of the idea of meaning in disease. It is said that every disease has a meaning. Another point of view, of great anthropological depth, consists in affirming that disease is always to be found intrinsically bound up with life itself, in such a manner that previous happenings—crises in the life of the individual—are the causes of the disease.

Such an interpretation leads to confusion between disease and sin. There is no doubt but that sin can at times produce disease. The man who goes beyond the bounds of temperance in any order finds himself more exposed to damage to his organism than the man who remains temperate. Disease, however, manifests itself even in the most rigorously temperate of beings, because disease appears in order to remind us that our existence cannot be explained of itself, but needs a thread to link it with that which lies beyond.

Man is an "open" structure; it follows, therefore, that the postulate of his transcendency is inexcusable. This open character of human existence is revealed with particular plasticity in sickness. It follows that disease cannot have meaning without reference to the categories of liberty and transcendency. Sickness always supposes a reduction of the biological autonomy of a person; but it leaves intact his liberty to take up a position against it. This possibility of making a stand points to the existence of the soul.

To-day the world is permeated by the Utopian notion of indefinite progress. Disease reminds us of the Utopian character of such an idea because, while it is certain that the sick-rate is diminishing, that mortality figures are decreasing for many diseases, that the average length of life is increasing, and so on it is no less certain that every human life has, and must have, its end. Disease is an image of this limit of existence, death. Life can only be defined with reference to the inexorable presence of death.

And what does it mean, to cure, to restore health? Difficult as it is to distinguish between health and sickness, it is even more difficult to attempt to define what is meant by curing.

The curative action does not consist only in the aim of regaining, or actually re-establishing, the position before the illness. There are no steps backwards in human life. Illness is a crisis point in life, from which the personality can emerge with new horizons. The doctor is not merely the technician who applies a remedy or carries out an operation, but the man who, possessing certain knowledge and experience, looks after another man in an illness. The secret of psychotherapeutic cures lies in the process of transference; now, a similar transference, in a mitigated form, exists in every medical action, even the most trivial. From this follows the need for the doctor to be truly deserving of the transference which the patient projects on him; for this is nothing other than his means of dulling his anguish.

The doctor can never pay enough attention to this problem of the distress of his patients. The natural helplessness of the human creature makes itself most obvious in time of sickness. The doctor must handle the distress of his patients with more care than their most acute and intimate physical ills—because, at base, there lies the craving of the creature for something that surpasses it.

This is the reason why illnesses so frequently give rise to religious crises. Distress grows the more the disease threatens life.

Finally, I should like to remind Catholic doctors of a duty: that of perfection. There is no worse example than that of the incompetent Catholic professional man who not only tries to excuse his incompetence but even flaunts it as a sign of his detachment from the things of this world. "Scientific progress" said the Pope in his allocution to the Pax Romana Congress held in Amsterdam in 1950 "cannot, as such, disturb the believer, who rather takes pleasure in serving it and who hails in every discovery a shining manifestation of the wisdom and grandeur of the Creator." And a little further on he adds: "In these conditions, Christian students and intellectuals, you should participate each according to your vocation in the work of the Redemption in the world that is

59

being born before our eyes. In effect, does not co-operation in this work for health require that you should place yourselves in the very heart of contemporary intellectual efforts, in the image of Christ, like to us in everything, except sin?"

II

ART IN THE TECHNOLOGICAL AGE

Ann Blyth, although still in her twenties the star of more than thirty major motion pictures, climbs inevitably towards Hollywood Academy honour as film-land's best actress. Some already think her current characterisation in The Helen Morgan Story may bring her 1958's Oscar.

Vibrant and versatile, Miss Blyth has achieved equal distinction as a star in light opera, musical comedy and classical drama. Her talents have been given generously and energetically to many good causes. Catholic film, television and radio programmes, notably Father Peyton's "Family Theatre" and Fr. James Keller's "The Christophers", have been faithfully and constantly served by Miss Blyth, whose ready patronage has enhanced their public prestige as national Catholic movements with international affiliates.

In private life Ann Blyth is the devoted wife of Dr. James McNulty, brilliant young Hollywood obstetrician, who is a brother of musical star Dennis Day. The McNultys were married four years ago by James Francis Cardinal McIntyre, at the Church of St. Charles Borromeo in North Hollywood. Their beautiful home, sedately artistic and in no sense a typical Hollywood film-star show place, is now enlivened by two delightful children, Timothy, aged three, and Maureen, who is one and a half.

Between the private life of Ann McNulty, wife and mother, and the public life of Ann Blyth, vivacious film star, there exists a barrier of healthy reserve, but the devout Catholicism which shines in the one lends brighter light to the other.

In striving to paraphrase Miss Blyth one does violence to her simple directness, sharp wit and warm, personal charm. Out of natural modesty Miss Blyth, in turn, does herself injustice.

For this reason you will find in her remarks no reference to many interesting instances of Catholic Action, relevant to her career in the films. Ann Blyth, more often than any other Catholic I know in Hollywood, by example or reflection has lifted the intentionally risqué situation from its rut; turned the ugly thought upwards towards beauty.

William H. Mooring, her interviewer, was born in England, December 1898, of rural stock. He was baptized and in 1921 married in an English village church built by Catholics in A.D. 1080.

Small-town reporter and film critic, later London trade journal editor and eventually assistant to the director of production at British International Studios, England, Mooring first visited Hollywood in 1932 to assist production of Noel Coward's Cavalcade, award-winning film of 1933. In 1934, accompanied by his wife, son and daughter, he returned to Hollywood as a columnist-reporter for British national newspapers.

In 1940 the Moorings together received the gift of faith, and were baptized by the Rev. Cornelius J. McCoy, S.J. at the Church of the Blessed Sacrament, Hollywood. In 1943 Mooring relinquished secular for Catholic journalism. Since 1944 he has syndicated a weekly column, "Hollywood In Focus", and service of television and film reviews, now appearing in forty-six Catholic publications throughout the U.S.A and Canada.

A Catholic Actress Looks at the Motion Picture

ANN BLYTH

in an interview with William H. Mooring

It is a privilege to be chosen from among the many Catholics in the film and television industries of Hollywood to present a few thoughts for consideration on the occasion of the Second World Congress for the Lay Apostolate.

One is warned that every privilege carries upon its back its own weight in moral responsibility. I am especially mindful of this as I share these pages with eminent Catholic scholars, scientists, world leaders and men of letters. For if my views should gain a measure of acceptance—or evoke some mild challenge—they can do so only as those of an individual Catholic actress who speaks her own mind, frankly, yet humbly aware that none among us may speak for all.

We are to look, I am told, at the Catholic actress's approach to her career, in the light of her individual conscience. We are to face some of her (or his) problems in reconciling personal contributions to the motion picture art with personal responsibilities to Christian morality. In a still larger sense we are to define some of the responsibilities and opportunities of the individual Catholic artist towards and in motion pictures and television as subtly powerful instruments in the formation of world-wide public opinion.

I must at once say that this seems a very large order for one little person to fulfil!

We may find, perhaps, a fairly solid starting point in certain widely accepted generalities. From the start the motion picture has grown like a thriving child. Television has now given it, if not new and sharper eyes, at least new perspectives in which to search the worldly scene. Various influences have come to shape and reshape the artistic forms and commercial policies of the motion picture as a universal medium of communication.

Most significantly, within recent years, World War II, with its wide sweep of human suffering, social disruption and political and economic upheaval, was reflected on the screen via so-called dramatic "neo-realism". During the ensuing years of "cold war", even up to the present time, this kind of influence has been increasingly apparent in some of the more challenging and interesting examples of screencraft sent to us here in America from various countries in Europe and even Asia.

Not all these films have appealed at once to American tastes and interests. Some, by reason of obscure themes or particular emphasis upon sordid detail, have proved unrewarding, even repellent, to general audiences in the U.S.A. The overall effect, however, of the "neo-realistic" cult, if one may use the word advisedly, is now strongly apparent. Imported films, when not widely booked in American theatres, now frequently gain public attention via television which brings them even closer into the sharing of ideas with the American family. The twofold outlet of theatre and fireside, quickened in sentimental and emotional interest by those wartime contacts and postwar alliances which strengthen American-European friendships, has built up public appeal for good imported motion pictures. In turn this has stimulated further a Hollywood search for more realism in its own film drama; a trend started here and elsewhere as a natural consequence of the violent experiences of war.

Competition has sharpened also between those making films solely for theatres and others catering to that voracious youngster, television. This new competitive spirit has led to increased specialization. Older methods and systems used during an era of Hollywood mass production have been revamped or discontinued. There are now, within the Hollywood production system as a whole, many more small, self-contained production units than ever before. Each of these is under the direction of an alert and usually young creative executive, or a small group of such men. Each has a specialized interest in one particular film production at a time. As one successful young writer-producer told me recently: "We are now turning out screenplays, not sausages!"

The effect of these changes upon the individual artist, whether he be a producer, director, writer or actor, is self-evident. He must no longer seek success on a continuing basis through stereotypes or clever improvisation on formulae already publicly approved. The public demands change, change and more change. The individual technician or artist may therefore exercise to-day greater freedom in self-expression and self-determination. He does so, however, only under correspondingly greater responsibility to the industry employing him and the banking interests which stand behind it. To-day in the film business, we see that the commercial gamble is greater than ever before: the competition in personal talent correspondingly keener.

How does this trend affect the individual Catholic within the film and television arts? The solving of inevitable conflicts between career and conscience has always been and must probably ever remain an entirely individual matter for the Catholic artist himself to decide. One naturally assumes with readiness that the true Catholic artist desires above all else to utilize his art in the service of an ideal. Here one turns instinctively to our Holy Father, Pope Pius XII. Speaking to members of the Italian motion picture industry in July 1955, His Holiness said (of "the ideal film"): "Some deny that an absolute ideal can exist. In other words they affirm that the ideal is a relative concept, meaning something only for a definite person or thing." While affirming that "the ideal will always be found in something absolute which is verified in every case", His Holiness added that the ideal film must be considered under three aspects:

(1) In relation to the spectator to whom it is directed.

(2) In relation to the content of the film.

(3) In relation to the community upon which it exercises a particular influence.

One sees how, with inspired wisdom, the Holy Father guides our thoughts towards the practical issues, and the personal solutions presented.

One Catholic actor may, by the particular characteristics of his talent, find himself frequently, perhaps even constantly, exposed to a choice of screenplays giving rise in various ways to moral questions. Another actor, whose forte lies in a different, perhaps lighter, type of screen character, may seldom face a difficult decision.

While individual conflict must be resolved in the personal conscience, the Holy Father's words seem to indicate that collective application of Catholic principles provides a final safeguard. Few, if any, of Hollywood's actors, or even for that matter the producers of the films themselves, can have any very clear indications as to the audiences their films are to reach once they are made. However scrupulous any of us may tend to be in these matters, once individual conscience has been properly exercised in relation to the moral content of a particular screenplay in the written form, once it takes the final form of image and sound upon film, all moral sanctions pass to others who must decide to what type of spectator the film shall be directed. Here, quite clearly, is where Catholic classification of motion pictures, and discriminating Catholic selection of programmes, have their beginning. The responsibility of parents concerning motion picture and television dramatizations their children shall or shall not see, is quite firmly fixed. The content of a film may involve realistic exploration of human degradation through immorality. The character one must play may be a wanton sinner. There may be in the story no improvised triumph of right over wrong. Indeed, it is a characteristic of many recent screenplays that the moral verities are reflected as a part of a general

67

presentation, not as a sudden, emphatic, climatic resolution. The obvious in moral compensation no longer coincides with the ultimate in dramatic conviction.

The ideal is to be determined in the individual instance, according to a clear understanding of character and circumstance, properly informed by Christian conscience.

His Holiness also told the Italian film producers—and his words must surely apply to all who participate in the production of motion pictures—"Everyone knows that there is no difficulty at all in producing seductive films by making them accomplices of the lower instincts and passions."

In the same speech however, the Holy Father acknowledged "the tremendous dynamic activity to which the cinema has given life" and, too, "the unusually wide and deep influence in the thinking, the habits, the life of countries where it develops its power, particularly among the poorest classes, for whom the cinema is often the sole recreation after work, and among youth, who see in the motion picture a quick and attractive means of quenching the natural thirst for knowledge and experience."

The Catholic artist, whatever the limits of his influence, is unlikely to escape conscientious reminders of his Christian duty. In Hollywood, as elsewhere, dramatic criticism and direct public reaction sharpen his awareness of the tremendous scope and impact of new sciences in communication which have come to the service of his art.

This awareness of public criticism cannot in the first place immunize him against errors of professional or moral judgment. Still, good faith towards the public, a sense of responsibility towards the industry which employs him, and well-formed Christian intentions—these first principles of Catholic ethics and morals are more evident in Hollywood than may sometimes be apparent on the surface.

If one may inject personal experience by way of illustration, I would express some pleasure in these facts. It has been my happy experience to enjoy a measure of success on the screen. Of more enduring significance, I am richly blessed in my private life as Mrs. James McNulty. For a devoted husband and two adorable children I am humbly grateful to divine Providence.

For my comparative success with the public I should perhaps give some of the credit to shrewd management. I have been starred in many screenplays of a non-controversial type, although some of you may recall my earlier characterization of the rebellious daughter in *Mildred Pierce* and the young woman wrongly condemned for murder in *Thunder on the Hill*. These provided sharp contrasts to the devout little girl I played in *Sally and St. Anne*, the lively heroines in *Rose Marie* and *The Student Prince*, and Bing Crosby's little partner in *Top o' the Morning*, to mention just a few films in passing.

One learns that to switch from lighter to more tensely dramatic story material inevitably means that some segments of the public will approve while others do not. This reaction may be due principally to natural differences in public taste. There is, however, a strong tendency here in the U.S.A to classify all films in one of two general types. Anything light and airy is apt to be regarded as purely "escapist" while the label "realistic" is indiscriminately applied to almost any dramatic effort in which occurs the slightest exploration of character. Correspondingly there is a tendency to identify escapism with superficiality and to recognize artistic maturity and integrity only where the ultimate in dramatic realism is apparent.

On the subject of superficiality in entertainment, His Holiness, while referring to "the ideal film", said: "It is not being denied that even a somewhat superficial entertainment can rise to artistic levels and be classed as ideal, since man has his shallows as well as his depths". Just as quickly I would recall the Holy Father's conclusion: "Dull is the man who is entirely superficial." This I would paraphrase if I might: "Dull is the actor who must ever play the same role!"

At the present time I am impersonating one of the celebrated figures of popular American entertainment, the late

Helen Morgan, in a film biography which Michael Curtiz is directing for Warner Brothers.

The Helen Morgan Story presents for me something of a challenge. Miss Morgan lived recently enough to be remembered by large segments of the public. Her private life was a full one, invaded, here and there, by characters of the criminal underworld. My choice of a story in which I am seen as a public figure whose private life was not in all respects as endearing as her personal charm, has evoked minor protests, mainly from among those who prefer to see me in light comedy or musicals.

These comments, although not particularly representative, are perhaps indicative. They seem to illustrate the insistence on the part of at least some film-goers that an actress and the characters she consents to play cannot be viewed apart. A few American admirers have asked, with a trace of hurt, how I can bring myself to drop the characteristic sweetness with which they credit me, in order to portray a woman who, among other things, died an alcoholic. My answer, as may be readily understood in your countries, is that the cause behind this sad case of human disintegration gives the story its deep human interest and purpose. Helen Morgan, in this screenplay, is not only the wonderful artist who sang her songs from the top of a piano. She is the Helen Morgan to whom the cards of life seemed to be dealt from the lower deck; who yearned for affection and understanding, even trying in desperation to buy friendship with extravagant largesse. It was the compassionate quality of the story as well as the opportunities inherent in the characterization that led me into this part. I am quite confident that my choice was a wise one and that when the film reaches the screen even those who now doubt this will agree.

If one may once again quote from the Holy Father's thesis on "the ideal film" one finds counsel in these words, "It [the ideal film] does not make an empty show of moralizing, but it more than makes up for this by positive work which, as circumstances demand, instructs, delights, diffuses genuine and noble joy and pleasure and cuts off every approach to boredom."

One is to strive, then, towards achieving in one's work the quality which His Holiness concludes "will beguile in such a manner that the spectator, at the conclusion, leaves the hall more light-hearted, relaxed and, within himself, better than he entered."

Here then is the admonition. It is the part of the Catholic artist to strive always towards compliance.

This is the share in the great work of the lay apostolate to which every Catholic actor, director, producer and writer is called. Not all may feel worthy but all, not least your humble servant, will presume upon your prayers.

Hermann Baur was born in Basle (Switzerland) on 25th August, 1894. He studied under Prof. Moser and began his career as an architect in France.

His work includes many important edifices of his home town: schools, a hospital and a housing scheme for some 1500 inhabitants, and a series of churches: in Basle (All Saints' Church and St. Michael's), in other Swiss towns (the Church of St. Nicholas of Flue in Bern, St. Mary's in Olten, etc.), in France (Hem and Cahagnes), Germany (Grenzach) and the Saar (Thailen).

Visiting Professor of the Swiss Federal University of Technology, Hermann Baur is a member, and was for many years President, of the Federation of Swiss Architects; a member of the International Congresses for Modern Architecture, and of the Schweizerischer Werkbund and the Societas Sancti Lucae. He has been frequently called upon as a lecturer in Switzerland and neighbouring countries.

What Does the Modern World Expect from Christian Art?

HERMANN BAUR

It must be said quite frankly and unequivocally that recently the human search and longing for some sort of emotional, non-rational expression of the religious life went on for more than a century without finding any satisfactory response. Nietzsche's outburst, that Christians would have to sing better hymns before he could begin to believe anything of what they said, was undoubtedly, whatever else it may have been, a cry from the heart. The voice of any real and vital *ars sacra* was absolutely silenced, and what gave itself out as such had become no more than a pitiful artificial substitute. Because of all the worries lying so heavily upon the Church in those days, a long time passed without there being any clear realization of the disadvantages that must inevitably arise from such a situation. People ignored the fact that man's religious needs cover not only his reason but his emotional life and his senses too. What took place in the nineteenth century meant, fundamentally, an invasion into the Church's own sphere of that very kind of rationalism which she had always condemned; the kind that held that the sort of knowledge that could be taken in by the intellect should be regarded almost exclusively as the sole valid one. Only the slightest attention was paid to that beauty which St. Thomas had described as a reflection of inner truth and goodness. People seemed to have lost all sense of that kind of radiance that can still be active and effective upon the hearts and wills of men long after rational argument has lost its power of appeal.

And yet the whole history of the Church and church art

constitutes resounding proof of this fact; the magnificent expressions of the inner essence of the Christian religion, which are to be found in such profusion in the artistic works of the Christian era until the beginning of the nineteenth century, still provide many people with their one last link with the Church and may sometimes be the first thing that attracts them towards her. But precisely this "backwards" way of looking at the matter, this connection with the Church as something merely surviving from the past, is bound to be unsatisfying and in the last resort even dangerous. It provides all too easy an excuse for those people who do indeed respect what the Church has done in the past but regard all this as dwelling in the unrepeatable good old days—and thereby do the Church the greatest of all wrongs.

With the onset of the twentieth century an increasing number of voices were raised in a demand for a kind of art and culture that should be the product of our own life and times. "The Church must enter into every earthly form, for she has been sent to sanctify the world, which finds its fulfilment in time": these words, spoken by a German, like the clarion calls sounded by Karl Muth, Jacques Maritain and Paul Claudel, were regarded increasingly as expressing a clear obligation, and gradually the bastions that were raised against a vital modern art are being overturned. In Catholic literature questions of contemporary art and culture are once again taking their traditional place. Highly significant of the change that has been accomplished in this field are the writings of the Trappist, Thomas Merton, who says, in his *Figures for an Apocalypse*: "But a genuine aesthetic experience is something which transcends not only the sensible order (in which, however, it has its beginning) but also that of reason itself. It is a suprarational intuition of the latent perfection of things. Its immediacy outstrips the speed of deduction and leaves all analysis far behind."

At once liberated and stimulated by this new perception, a new spring of Christian art burst into being. Catholic creative artists who wanted to be more than Catholic in the narrow sense became acknowledged figures in the great wide world of literature—Léon Bloy, Paul Claudel, Georges Bernanos, Graham Greene, Reinhold Schneider and the rest. In the works of these writers the Church's position, her timeless and yet at the same time so timely mission, using all the means of the immediate present, was clearly restated. And lo! the world, the so-called modern world, pricked up its ears and listened; the message had reached hearts that had been believed to be far from and firmly proof against all things religious. It was as though they had been waiting for this "new song" to come from the inner recesses of the Church.

No less powerful was the awakening of *ars sacra* in the plastic arts. As the author of the present paper is more closely connected with these than he is with literature (or music) he is able to go into this matter a little more closely. The rupture between the Church and genuine art perhaps appeared even more clearly in this field than in any other, and had been more deeply felt. "She is so lovely within, and all her exterior manifestations are so ugly," wrote Jean Marie Dulac of the Church, and of the church buildings of his day Paul Claudel said that they would "arouse remorse and horror like a difficult confession". In fact it is well-nigh impossible to estimate the loss experienced by the Church as a result of this refusal to contemplate the vital art of the times. Not a single work by the great painters of the nineteenth century—Cézanne, Van Gogh, Gauguin, not even Rouault, despite the fact that his whole life's work was Christian in inspiration—found its way into any of the churches of the day. The few exceptions—Puvis de Chavannes, for instance—only go to prove this lamentable rule.

With the suddenness almost of a thunderclap, however, a change set in here in France, the home of modern art, after the Second World War. The world discovered with astonishment that into a certain church—and quite a humble one, too, in Assi in Upper Savoy—works by such well-known, even famous, painters as Bonnard, Léger, Lurçat, Rouault and Richier had found their way. One hardly knows which to

75

admire more, the fact that these great painters, who had
seemed to all appearances to be so remote from the Church,
should have come forward at the first summons and given
the Church the best they could produce, or the fact that such
a thing had become possible on the Church's side. We need
to be grateful from the bottom of our hearts to the people who
were originally responsible for this epoch-making achievement—and that means above all the Dominicans and the
Paris review *Art Sacré*. For if anything at all is certain it is the
fact that they thereby restored the whole contact between art
and the Church, not only in this particular field but in a far
more general way. Soon came more no less astonishing
things: Matisse in his ripe old age filled the chapel at Vence
near Nice with the creations of his own now purified art, and
Fernand Léger crowned his life's work as a painter with his
highly expressive church windows at Audincourt, finished
shortly before his death. The "world" has reacted with
increasing enthusiasm to this new meeting between the
Church and great art. Perhaps it has mainly been rather a
kind of amazement, and a respect for the courage which has
manifested itself in this event; but the influence of these
recent works upon those who contemplate them will grow
deeper and more fundamental as time goes by, for they will
show in a wordless but compelling way, even in distant times
to come, that the Church is always a living thing.

Church architecture too, "the mother of the plastic arts",
has responded to the cry of St. Thomas Aquinas: "Give way,
O you outmoded things, let all things be made new!" This
process started less sensationally, but it had begun, by comparison, much earlier. After the First World War there arose
near Paris two church buildings by Perret in which reinforced concrete, the modern building material *par excellence*, was used to support the structure. In 1925 Karl Moser
built the church of St. Antony in Basle in Switzerland, and
Dr. Georg Schmidt, the well-known art critic, wrote at the
time that with this the Church had returned to the great
tradition of the Middle Ages. Whereupon there followed,

especially in Switzerland and Germany, a whole series of church buildings all taking their form from the material and spiritual data of their own day, free from the shackles of outmoded fashions and conventions. They were structures of the utmost simplicity and directness: from the Corpus Christi church in Aachen, the St. Karl in Lucerne, the Church of the Holy Sacrament in Dornach, a quite considerable series of churches has since arisen. The simple and concentrated style which is their distinguishing feature has opened up the way to a world which had previously stood over against the Church in an attitude of indifference or hostility—a fact which could be substantiated by remarks made by many distinguished non-Catholics. The world-wide repercussion aroused by one of the most recent works, the Pilgrims' Church in Ronchamp, may have a slight element of the sensational about it, but all things considered, even this may be taken as a sign that church architecture is about to recover its old prestige and that the building of churches is again becoming a sort of mission, moving people to an awareness of ultimate things with the power of what is true and vital that still slumbers even in modern man.

This mission will not present itself, of course, with the magnificence of the *Ecclesia Triumphans* as it did in the Middle Ages and the time of the Baroque. The churches of our day cannot be expected to dominate our towns like Gothic cathedrals. But there is no cause for alarm in that. Is the Papacy, for instance, any less great for having concentrated, since it was relieved of all temporal power, on purely spiritual and religious matters? In the same way the impact made by the artistic side of church building depends far less than is generally supposed on material dimensions, and its power to move is to be found to-day mainly in its concentration upon what is essential and genuine. The thing that marks church building off from all other kinds of building and emphasizes its sacred character is its difference from the everyday. Church interiors of to-day must take us right away from the busy-ness of active life, must encourage us to concentrate and recollect ourselves, and raise us inwardly so that we are in a state to receive the Gospel tidings and gain some sense of the communion of the saints. This is why all the best churches of our day are places whose atmosphere is calm and withdrawn; anything noisy, anything that can distract one's attention, is eschewed, and the slanting light comes in subduedly in a way that draws the mind and senses to the centre piece of the whole construction, the altar. In no other place can modern man experience this inner elevation so intensely as he can inside a church, and nowhere else will artists—painters, sculptors and architects—find such an opportunity for expressing the profound and the sublime.

In the clarity and stillness of modern churches modern man can again get some idea of what the house of God really is and what really takes place inside it. The service, the liturgy—whose revival is a matter of such great interest to the Church—will be able to reach such perfection in modern churches that it will not be without its effect even upon those who stand outside, because the elementary forms which they embody now appear once again in their original purity. When, in former days, Romanesque simplicity threatened to degenerate into an excess of "decoration", St. Bernard of Clairvaux determined upon a return to a stricter and purer form of architecture. To-day perhaps we face a similar situation. Those romantic people who sigh after the venerable forms of former days and the eternal pessimists who can see nothing but dangers and errors everywhere do the Church a serious disservice. Can they not see that there is a new spirit abroad? Can they not see the vast gulf between the present and the things of yesterday, and can they not see how the best spirits of to-day are looking, even if only through a tiny crack, towards things that the Church, that great enemy of all materialism, has to offer them out of her treasury of signs and symbols?

A most felicitous co-operation has arisen between those who are called upon to fill the Church's life and liturgy with new life and the artists who have agreed to be taken into

78

the Church's service. It is being conducted seriously and with a proper sense of responsibility. Of course questions and problems arise that have to be handled carefully. The artist is always faced with the question as to how far he *dare* get away from the conventional without losing contact with the real tradition, and how far he *must*, so as to find really solid ground for his new type of construction. This and many other problems have all to be considered.

To those critics who hurl their *a priori* theological thunderbolts against this modern Christian art one might reply, in the words of Père Régamey: "If you had the simplicity of the Gospels you would be quiet." So let people stop and consider whether they are in a position to say anything on this subject, and if so to what extent, or whether they may not simply be clinging to old prejudices—prejudices which it must be said, are quite understandable, and which the artists themselves had first to overcome. On closer inspection, what is firmly and unshakeably good turns out far less often than one usually thinks to be hostile to all that lies in the future. Thus the charge is made against so-called abstract painting that it runs contrary to the Christian spirit. And yet this particular genre, the representation of abstract concepts, has had the right of entry into Christian churches from time immemorial —one has only to think of Byzantine and Ottonian art, not to speak of music or even architecture, which are essentially abstract arts. The *Biblia pauperum* of the Middle Ages was one, but not the only, form of plastic expression. The world is waiting for the Church's "new song", which can also ring out in certain works of abstract painting. Anyone who knows the abstract religious works by Alfred Manessier and has succumbed to his "Evening Litany", his "Passion According to St. John", his variations of the "Alleluia" theme, simply cannot understand the people who attack this form of art. These are to be found not least amongst educated people, who should try to remember that they bear a responsibility in this matter which they cannot simply evade by falling back on personal likes and dislikes.

It is also said that this kind of art is not generally comprehensible and that one should try to come down to the level of the average man. This argument too fails to stand up to closer scrutiny. (Besides which, if it was carried to its logical conclusion it would mean that art always had to descend to the lowest level.) The oft-repeated comparison with preaching does not hold water either: the preacher's word fades away as soon as it is spoken, while pictures remain, giving the watcher time to look at them in different moods. And then—and this is in fact the decisive point—pictures are not primarily directed at the intellect but at the heart and the feelings—and who will dare to say which of us is the more sensitive in these matters? Is it not simply a fact that, whether educated or not, not everyone can see equally deeply into a work of art? It would be ludicrous to imagine that the creators of the great works of Christian art in the past intentionally lowered their sights to the level of an "understanding" mass. Such a thing is quite unthinkable.

Hans Urs von Balthasar, in his *Schleifung der Bastionen*, says, optimistically: "Not perhaps for centuries has the Church's position been so full of promise, so open and pregnant for the future." Let us try not to let him down. A world in travail, the new world that is coming into being now, is looking to the Church for bold things, strong things. This persisting along old-fashioned roads, whether out of ignorance or self-interest or mere smugness, can lead nowhere except to that indifference which God "spews out of his mouth". Only a Christian art rising up resplendent, as boldly and blindingly as on the first day, will make it possible to penetrate into the soul of modern man and touch him to the quick.

*World Crisis from a Roman
Watchtower*

Count Wladimir Olivier-Marie-François de Paule Lefèvre d'Ormesson was born on 2nd August 1888, in St. Petersburg, where his father was Councillor at the French Embassy. After completing his studies in political science, he served throughout the war of 1914-18. In 1937 he was President of the Catholic Journalists' Guild. In May 1940 he was sent as Ambassador to the Holy See, but he was withdrawn from his post in October 1940 and, in February 1941, eliminated from all official activity by the Vichy Government. After the Liberation, he resumed his diplomatic career, and was sent, in May 1945, as Ambassador to Buenos Aires. The following year a special mission took him to Chile, and in March 1948 he returned to Rome as Ambassador to the Holy See and exercised these functions with outstanding success until he retired in September 1956.

As a journalist, Wladimir d'Ormesson has contributed to Figaro, *the* Revue de Paris, *the* Temps *and the* Journal de Genève. *His books include* Confiance en l'Allemagne? *and* Qu'est-ce qu'un Français? *and the autobiographical* Enfances diplomatiques.

An officer of the Legion of Honour, Wladimir d'Ormesson was elected on 3rd May 1956 to the Académie Française, taking the place left vacant by Paul Claudel.

World Crisis from a Roman Watchtower

WLADIMIR D'ORMESSON

Surprise is sometimes expressed in certain circles at the prominent part which notoriously Catholic politicians or parties of Christian inspiration played in Europe immediately after the War. The fact that Chancellor Adenauer, Alcide de Gasperi, Robert Schuman and Georges Bidault were simultaneously in power; that the CDO, the Christian Democrats and the *Mouvement Républicain Populaire* dominated or penetrated public life in Federal Germany, Italy and France, is viewed with suspicion in many quarters. "Vatican Europe. ..." How often we have heard the slogan! Rather than harking back to it perpetually without examining the facts which gave rise to it, it would be better to reflect on the reasons which did indeed bring Catholic principles and personalities to the fore at a dramatic moment of history.

For the second time in a generation, Europe was emerging from a fratricidal war, weak from loss of blood, in a state of ruin and chaos. This war had been let loose by pagan ideologies: contempt for promises and for human dignity, the cult of brute force, of race and the nation. Such were the mainsprings of this attempt at domination. As justice, in the long run, is always strongest, this explosion of pride ended as it should have ended. Was it not natural, then, especially in the countries where the explosion had taken place, that the peoples should turn, by reaction and instinctively, towards those who not only bore no responsibility for these disasters, but whom the vanquished and fallen régimes had overwhelmed with their sarcasm and pursued with their hatred? If declared Catholics led Federal Germany and Italy after the War (the case of France is different), and if Christian political parties played a decisive role in the countries which had to be saved from the wreckage, it was because the break-down of a materialistic civilization based on man's pride restored the primacy to Christian civilization based on the Gospel law of love. The rise to power of these men and these political groups was simply the victory of moral force over brute force. What finer homage could be rendered to the Papacy than to speak in this case of "Vatican Europe"? Do those who repeat the formula with hostility realize their own illogicality?

What has happened in the U.S.S.R has, moreover, only confirmed the truth of these statements. For it might have been hoped that, as a result of the terrible happenings of the war, Soviet Russia, at first the accomplice of Hitler's Third Reich and later the object of its attacks, would have learned its lesson. This, however, was not the case. The German-Soviet war was nothing more than a duel between wild beasts. And scarcely was it over when Stalin's dictatorship proved more terrible than ever. Europe split immediately in two. Its western half tended towards unification, precisely because it remained faithful to the reinstated principles of Christian civilization.

But, with the passing of time, the Western nations became reassured, and, becoming reassured, they tended to forget the abyss from which they were emerging and who had helped them to emerge. "When the danger is past, the saint is gobbled up", according to a proverb of ours—which comes from Italy! But, if too many people have too short memories, they make also another mistake: they do not see beyond their shadow. If they looked a little further, if they really thought of what is happening on the other side of the grim "iron curtain", they would realize their responsibilities—those of to-day and those of to-morrow. "We all know we shall die, but we don't believe it," said Joubert. We all know that freedom has ceased to exist in part of Europe—and in one half of the world. But do we really believe this dread reality? Do we imagine what it means in daily life? Do we make the effort to put ourselves in the place of these unhappy peoples? Because we are not suffering under it ourselves, do we not grow accustomed to their slavery? Do we not almost tend— out of weariness—to consider it as something natural?

No one, however, can become accustomed to living without the freedom he has once known. Tyranny is accepted because one cannot do otherwise. Sooner or later, when circumstances permit, man reclaims his rights. Already certain events in Central Europe have cast a gleam of light upon this darkness. A day will come—I do not know when— it may be far off, it may be nearer than we think, but inevitably a day will come, I am absolutely certain—when the "iron curtain" will collapse for good and the enslaved peoples will regain their freedom. When that day dawns, the Western world will see to its amazement that behind this screen there were scarcely any Communists; that our old Latin countries of the West had the strong minorities of Communist believers.

This will be a decisive moment for Europe. It will not, and must not, be a moment of revenge for old methods and selfish interests. On the contrary, it will be the opportunity for establishing in this vast European sector—and, if possible, beyond it—an order where just social claims and eternal spiritual and moral principles will be closely associated. In a word, it will be the hour of true Christian civilization. This hour will certainly strike; the hour of justice always does, sooner or later. Our duty is to prepare its coming.

SOCIAL SOLIDARITY: A CHRISTIAN DUTY

So it is that, yesterday in one part of Europe, to-morrow, be it sooner or later, in another part of Europe—and beyond it—the principles of Christian civilization have resumed, or will resume, their full significance. This is not only because war strewed the Continent with material and moral devastation. It is also because a new world is coming into being, because human society is undergoing an unprecedented upheaval, because everything needs rethinking, for everything is in transformation.

Why does the term "social" play such a part in our vocabulary? For certain very definite reasons: the mass civilization which has developed; the great human agglomerations which call for a more organized existence; the industrial centres, giving birth to collective activity; the elimination of distance; and finally, modern warfare, which is no longer a clash between troops but a collective undertaking of entire nations. In this transformation of social structures, the Christian is confronted with urgent problems. His duty of solidarity is put to the test, and becomes a torment for his conscience.

What is a Christian? One who, believing in God and in Christ, has received the command which alone contains "all the law and the prophets": "Thou shalt love the Lord thy God and thy neighbour as thyself." The Christian sounds his conscience. Can he remain indifferent and inactive when, day by day, more equitable social conditions are being devised? Is it not his duty, and the very reason for his existence, to be in the forefront of this activity; to ensure that collective existence, while unavoidable, will remain in conformity with the principles of the individual conscience? Does he not feel consternation at the sight of an immense part of modern society—precisely the part most closely affected by this collective existence—which regards him, if not as an enemy, at least as a stranger? Does he not then realize the responsibility incurred in the initial stages of industrial civilization, when his predecessors failed to understand that he should immediately integrate himself with this new form of social life; follow the peasant who left his village to become city-dweller and factory-worker; transport to the working suburb the village church progressively deserted by its parishioners; introduce the Gospel precepts, and make them operative, in these new fields of labour? Is he not distressed to ascertain all that has been lost to Christianity; the misconceptions, the misunderstandings, the antagonisms which have arisen—and, in the long run, the evil which has resulted for both sides? Is it too late now to turn the tide? Too late? The words are almost a blasphemy. It is never too late for anything. And so it is that, after the trials of another war, which was one of moral, more even than of material, destruction, we are witnessing to-day an admirable Catholic movement: Hierarchy, clergy, lay apostolate and Catholic intellectuals, aware of their responsibilities, are striving boldly—in some cases, even with heroic self-sacrifice—to pierce, as it were, the curtain of indifference, if not of hostility, which has fallen between the working class and the Church; their action is a reminder for all that Christ came to bring a law of love for all mankind.

How can we rest when we see the immense sum of misery still existing in and around so many of our cities? How resign ourselves to the sight of this inhuman congestion of human beings, these inexcusable slums and the pitiful children growing up in them? How can we accept the fact that so many of the aged and infirm vegetate in miserable poverty at the close of their hard-working existence? How can we fail to understand those who refuse to be turned into human instruments by the very forms of industrial labour? To understand also the workers' legitimate desire for social betterment, and the justice of the collaboration necessary between capital and labour? In short, once a Christian has understood all the responsibility implied in his title, how can he help devoting himself with all his strength to the improvement of man's lot, especially if he is convinced—as he has the right to be—that, Christendom being founded on the brotherhood of love, no other civilization can be more effective in bringing happiness and peace?

WISE, BUT NOT TOO WISE

Yes, all that is true. But, we must never let ourselves be carried away by passion, even if the passion is pure as the angels. For, in every passion, there is an element of abstrac-

87

tion, and therefore of unreality, and so of blindness. Chesterton has spoken of Christian ideas which can go mad. To try to do everything, i.e., to do everything at once, is to risk a humiliating setback. Society was not born yesterday, nor the ambition to improve social conditions. To work for the happiness of the collectivity, for a more just distribution of property, to promote social justice and reconcile justice with freedom—are these ideas which our generation alone has discovered? That would be a silly claim, and a real display of ignorance. There are so many ways of being a Pharisee, even in our idealism. The truth is that real improvement in social conditions requires solid foundations. To set a state in disorder under pretext of renewal, is a disastrous business. To heap burdens, to the point of collapse, on the shoulders of the State is also to prepare a bitter future for those who expect to benefit from this substitution. For a primary duty of the State is to protect society against inflation, that rotten fruit of economic fecundity, whose tangled confusion first enriches, but later again impoverishes the poor. The State's first duty is to have a healthy, sound currency, to undertake only what it can really carry out, to supervise everything but not to administer everything—though real improvement in the lot of the working class will never be effected through mere expedients and adventures. An elementary duty of the State is to avoid chancy improvisations which in fact lead to confusion and disorder. To put it plainly: the State's first duty is to be in earnest. And the Christian's first duty, as regards social life, is also to be in earnest.

All that is true. But, if one should never be carried away by passion, however generous, one should never be carried away either by good sense. The danger in imagination is that it is often led by emotion. But the danger of good sense is lack of emotion. It is easy to slip into immobility. Let us be frank: are not selfish considerations often hidden away beneath the principles of obvious experimental commonsense? Is not self-interest at times disguised under arguments of a general nature? I have often noticed that the speaker who proclaims that every man should do his duty where his lot in life has placed him has generally no reason to complain about the lot which has fallen to himself! We must not give way, then, even in the name of the most righteous principles, to self-satisfied conformism, mistaking the shelter of basic truths for a docile acceptation of the *status quo*. We must act. Even those —especially those—whose noble concern it is to preserve what is to be preserved, must act. Whoever takes no action, preserves nothing. And to act, we must be forever imagining, conceiving, daring. We must keep on trying until the voice of reason calls a warning. And, if we halt then, let it not be to stop trying, but to adapt our effort to changing circumstances.'

Such is the dialogue between the two conceptions of the social problem. "Keep on going," cries one voice. "You'll fall," cries another. "Take breath, but keep on. ..." There is a certain pathos in the dialogue between men faced with their destiny. We find it in every order of reality related to the things of the spirit; particularly in the field of Christian thought. Is this anything new? Does it justify misgivings? Does it give grounds for uneasiness? Of course not. This is the clash which produces the spark of truth; this twofold tension brings us to the vital point, focus of aspirations and experience, to the point which contains Christian truth, itself a vital point between the things of the earth and those beyond. But this dialogue is more than ever imperative in a chaotic world, groping in the midst of ruins, change and hope. One condition is necessary, however, in order to reach this vital point. An element of transcendency must remain common to those who are seeking it. This element exists, and it is precisely the element which makes man what he is: his conscience.

If our conscience tells us, on the one hand, that generosity, enthusiasm and thirst for justice may not neglect the realities which make up collective existence, and on the other, that we must not only listen to time-honoured experimental wisdom in order better to promote man's wellbeing, to create, and again to create, and still to create—on this twofold condition, we have a reconciliation of supposedly contrary sentiments; and the effect is irresistible.

Does this amount to saying that the exercise of conscience is the condition of a civilization based on justice? And I think I may say that among Catholics (of whom we are speaking) there is no reason to fear that "conscience" is not protected against temptations which seek to draw us outside the limits of reality.

Because, thanks be to God, an ever-increasing number of Catholics desire with all their might to make Christianity, so to speak, overflow into social life—and into international life; because they are not resigned to letting Christ's message remain unheard by a whole sector of society, and in particular, in too large a section of the world of labour where those whom Christ most loved are toiling; because they want to clear up the misunderstanding which would make some people believe that the Church relegates the fulfilment of justice to the next life, and others that justice is only possible here below; because so many Catholics are trying to remain attuned to present-day living and to prove that their faith is more than ever a living reality; because these Catholics are on fire with faith, and so with charity—all of this is no reason for separating these sentiments from the strict idea they have of their duty; from the need they feel for discipline; from their loyalty to the teachings of the Supreme Magisterium; from their avowed certainty of the Church's indestructible unity; from the absolute obedience, filled not only with respect, but, if I may say so, with affection, which they profess towards the successor of the Apostle to whom Christ said: "Thou art Peter, and upon this rock I will build my Church", His Holiness Pius XII, gloriously reigning, the Pope of peace.

THE FUNCTION OF PAPAL ROME

Rarely in the course of history have the responsibilities of the Roman Pontiff been heavier with consequences. It is his task, indeed, if I may so put it, to set the pace of Catholicism in the upheaval of a world which is seeking a lost equilibrium.

One must perhaps have lived in Rome in order fully to grasp one of the essential attributes of the Church's Supreme Magisterium. For the Papacy is not only the head of the Mystical Body, which is the Church. It is not only the guardian, twenty centuries old, of the deposit of Catholic faith and revelation, a deposit which includes the Sacred Books of the Old and the New Testament and a tradition handed down from generation to generation up to the present day. It is also, if I may say so, the "cornerstone" of the most heterogeneous of all edifices. This heterogeneity is, moreover, perfectly natural, and constitutes the Church's strength. This Catholic Church, whose heart has been beating for twenty centuries in Rome, has spread over the whole world, across all frontiers of race and continent. But every nation and every human group has its own peculiar psychology. To bring together all these elements, often far removed one from the other, in one and the same religious discipline; to bring into step all these Churches which make up the Church—this is the supreme function of papal Rome. A twofold responsibility. On the one hand, in so far as is fitting, contingent circumstances and local shades of difference must be taken into account. On the other hand, nothing must be allowed to impede strict unity.

This constant readjustment is the object of constant effort on the part of the Papacy. It calls for uninterrupted attention and unequalled tact. Catholics themselves are not always aware of it. It is so difficult for them to grasp the meaning of their Church's universality. It is so human for governments, political parties and peoples to try to draw the Church each one to itself, to make use of her, to monopolize her. It is so usual for the Church's freedom to be attacked from all sides. The history of the Papacy is partly filled with this struggle, which has gone on, in different forms throughout the centuries: between the Papacy and Empire, between the Holy See and the nascent states, between the law of Christ and the excesses of nationalism. According to the times, it has been associated with Investitures, absolutism, Gallicanism, Febronianism, Josephism; with the civil constitution for the clergy; later, and in certain forms, with secularism; later again, with Fascism and National Socialism. It has led to schisms. It has divided the Christian world.

And yet, if the Church, because she is universal and because her kingdom is not of this world, is not and cannot be subjected to watertight compartments, of whatever kind, she knows too well the values of civilization not to pay honour to all that is necessary and sound in the national idea. This equilibrium, this vital point between the universal principles on which the Church is founded and the national principles without which the world would be doomed to anarchy, is tirelessly recalled by Pope Pius XII throughout his apostolate. We have only to reread the admirable "messages" the Sovereign Pontiff addressed to Christendom —and to the whole of mankind—on 10th November 1956, at Christmas 1956, and at Easter 1957. All the problems of the day are reviewed in these messages; and all are given the solution of eternal truth.

To sum up: we are living in a world of upheaval and distress. A new era is being built on the ruins of the old. A new equilibrium is being sought amidst dire misunderstandings. Mankind longs for peace and fails to achieve it. When he flies over the earth, he knows neither distance nor frontier, but as soon as he comes down to earth, he finds himself again in a split and divided universe, where partitions are more unyielding than ever and peoples more than ever shut off from one another. Science has placed in his hands new possibilities for creation, opening up almost unlimited perspectives. But, up to date, these discoveries seem directed largely towards destruction. If we do not want to be torn apart by these terrible contradictions, there must be a total revision of our ways of living and of thinking. We must think out anew the problem of man's lot.

In a society which—whether we like it or not—is assuming, and will assume, increasingly collective forms, is there not a capital distinction to be made, in the first place, between the equality of men and the identity of men?

Equality, by all means. That is to say, the equality of men before their Creator. Every man has his right to be a person, i.e., his right to his own soul. Every man has the duty to respect the person, i.e., the souls of others. Man's exploitation by man is a sin, not before men but before God.

But the identity of men is something different; for man is not a mechanical product. Every man is a created being. There will always be an immense diversity among men. Some will be strong, others weak, some enterprising, and some timid. There will always be born leaders, and there will always be followers. Which amounts to saying that there will always be men who will outstrip others, who will amass more riches than others, who will tend, as far as their carnal appetites are concerned, to exploit others.

This is where the need for discipline comes in, so that men's non-identity will not compromise what is just and even sacred in their equality. But there are two ways—and I can see only two—of ensuring this discipline.

One way consists in imposing the individual's duties towards the community by violence, police terror and the gag. Man's dignity is sacrificed in an abstract worship of mankind. A system of this kind can only be conceived, and above all can only be maintained, by tyranny.

The other way consists in imposing these duties by fostering a strict individual conscience. For us, as Christians, this means loyal observance of the laws of Christianity. For those who do not share our Christian faith, it means faith in a lofty religious ideal.

There is no other way out. Either man will remain bound to God, his Creator, to the infinite Principle, and will realize the duties this supernatural vocation imposes, not only towards himself, but towards his neighbour, who is created also by God. Or man will be nothing better than a robot.

And so we come to this conclusion: The more mankind progresses, the closer its unity, the more discoveries and technical inventions transform the conditions of its existence, the greater becomes its need of spiritual life. If man is to preserve his freedom, he must preserve his soul. When the body has grown, it needs a supplement of soul, as the thinker Henri Bergson wrote in the evening of his life. Yes, this carnal and material body has grown in relation to space and time. Human genius has accomplished wonders during these last decades. Like Prometheus, it has snatched from the mystery which envelops us some of its most extraordinary secrets. But if the soul which animates this body does not also grow, to embrace and purify the triumphs of technical progress and give them a higher meaning, the fate of Prometheus awaits us.

That is why the transitional period through which we are living, though beset with difficulties, filled with contradictions and rich in dramatic tensions, seems to me to be charged with exceptional interest. That is why we should face it, not with lamentations, but with enthusiasm. Tremendous labours await us. Tremendous responsibilities are ours. We must, indeed, meet them with wisdom, with clear-sighted reason and with the accumulated treasures of experience; but we must also accept them with imagination, with courage, with fortitude and with faith.

Such is the meaning of the lay apostolate.

III

THE WORLD COMMUNITY

Giorgio la Pira was born at Pozzale (Sicily) on 9th January, 1904, of a poor family. He studied by night and in all the free time left by his work for his father and his uncle, and later for a shoe-maker in Messina. Finally the boy's exceptional talent won the interest of his professor, who took him to Florence. At twenty-two he had graduated from the University and was Lector in Law; and at twenty-six, after specializing in Roman Law, he was appointed Professor.

Other responsibilities, however, awaited him. In 1946, he was elected to the first Italian Constituent Assembly, and in 1948 re-elected to Parliament. Later he was Secretary of State for Labour. Elected Mayor of Florence in 1951, he gave up his seat in Parliament to devote himself entirely to the city, "the flower of Christian civiliza-tion", and especially to the cause of its less privileged citizens. The "revolutionary" economic policy of the Mayor of Florence found its inspiration in the Gospels.

La Pira is perhaps best known to-day on account of the "Inter-national Congresses for Peace and Christian Civilization" which he initiated in Florence in 1952 and which have since attracted annually to his city representatives from all parts of the world. Each year a new theme was chosen: "Civilization and Peace"—"Prayer and Poetry" —"Culture and Revelation"—"Christian Hope and Human Hopes" —"History and Prophecy". In addition, a "Congress for Mayors of Capital Cities" brought together in Florence, in October 1955, the Lord Mayors of London, Paris, Moscow, Bucharest, New Delhi, Peiping. . . .

An active member of the St. Vincent de Paul Society, La Pira enlisted the ready help of the Society in Tuscany on behalf of the contemplative monasteries and convents for women in Italy, and later in Africa, Asia and throughout the world. He has accompanied this material help with a unique correspondence destined to create a closer link between the "power centres" of Christianity and those for whom their prayers and sacrifices are offered.

Among his published works are: The Value of the Human Person, Our Social Vocation, *etc.*

Unity in Diversity

GIORGIO LA PIRA

The tragic events which are causing turmoil in so many parts of the world, far from discouraging us and giving rise to scepticism, increase the need for grace and charity in our souls, and challenge us to raise our banner of hope higher than ever.

For, on the one hand, our Christian faith demands that we hope even when all hope seems dead (and it is far from dead to-day: for while it is true that the possibility of war is greater, it is also true that the possibility of lasting peace is far greater still). And, on the other hand, hope itself urges us to see the swing of present-day world history—in spite of all its internal disunity—as directed towards one fundamental end: that of advancing, and raising to a higher level of civilization and human dignity, the peoples and nations of whole continents, and thus setting up a new organic unity among all the peoples and nations of the world.

That the world of to-day is thus providentially full of possibilities is a fact for all to see. No one observant of present historical developments can deny it. And this inner, organic process of unification among all the peoples and nations of the world is moving to a rhythm that becomes daily more rapid. It is a unification that affects all the elements that make up the life of a nation: it is a unification in matters technological, economic, social, cultural, political, and, in the widest sense, religious. It affects all the civilizations now existing in the world, their foundations, their framework and their highest achievements.

But must it be a unification excluding all diversity? Is it to reduce the rich variety of feature and even structure of peoples, nations, and civilizations to a dull uniformity?

97

No indeed. Unity, yes, but unity in diversity: organic unity: all the branches live from the one trunk, but each has its own richness, each lives according to its own specific kind. We are many in one body.

This is, so to say, the theme that human history is working out in our time—a time shattered by manifold calamities, but yet rich in possibilities and hope for the future.

One need only cite what we may call the recent "historical discovery" of the peoples, nations and civilizations of Africa and Asia; these contemporary historical and political awakenings are, after the geographical discoveries of the late fifteenth century, one of the most significant facts of history. The latter gave its shape and meaning to the history of the last five hundred years of man's story; the former may perhaps give shape and meaning to the history of the third millenium which we can already begin to see taking shape in the distance; we can say with the Gospel: "Lift up your heads and see".

And even now these historical discoveries, and this process of unification which history is so rapidly effecting, are beginning to produce a real "revolution" in the criteria and practice of the political, economic, social and cultural life of the world: from now on, events cannot be validly measured upon any other than an intercontinental scale. No gauge limited to one continent can give any exact idea of the meaning, direction or end of what is now happening anywhere.

Europe is not an isolated continent any more; nor is America; each finds in the other continents—Asia, Africa, Oceania—the completion it needs in all spheres of ordinary human life, from the economic to the spiritual. The universal message of the Gospel comes to mind: "... and even to the uttermost part of the earth". (Acts i. 8.)

This "growth" of history, raising up new peoples and new nations to the highest levels of civilization, does not in any sense indicate any waning or slackening of the great mission to civilize and improve—spiritually, culturally, socially and technologically—entrusted to the West. Quite the reverse: it demands greater energy and more definite action, to enlighten all the peoples and nations of the world with that light which the Gospel has made the responsibility of the peoples and nations of the West, and which makes Europe—in spite of her inevitable deficiencies, limits and waywardness—in a sense both the womb and the measure of the highest civilization of mankind.

We need the courage to rekindle more brightly again today that light which opens to men the gates of brotherly love; that light which is at once divine and human; which gave birth to the *Summae* of theology and metaphysics; which gave birth to the cathedrals, wove the network of the monasteries; inspired the most exquisite beauty in poetry and art, built the most magnificent cities of the world; and which has attained, in science, economics and technology, quite undreamt-of levels of civilization.

To do this, the West must cleanse itself of the selfishness and atheism which stand in its way: it must return to the Christian love and faith whence it received its life and its "mission to serve" civilization. Only if it does this will it have nothing to fear from the tremendous historical advances that are bringing new peoples, nations and civilizations up to its own level to be given integration and power to act in their turn.

And here I should like, if I may, to support this vision of hope by referring to that fundamental mystery of the Christian faith—the Mystical Body. This mystery was revealed by Christ himself in the discourse after the Last Supper (John xv. 1; xvii. 21), and in a sense completed by Saint Paul who preached it so fervently.

This mystery signifies precisely the unity in Christ—the "incorporation" into Christ, as St. Paul says—of all nations excluding none: "That the Gentiles should be fellow-heirs, and of the same body, and co-partners." (Eph. iii. 6.)

All nations, then, are called to be members of a single body; all are called to the same inheritance of grace and truth; all are to be worked upon by the one divine leaven fermenting throughout the world.

What, then, has been, is and will always be the "theme" pursued by God in the history of mankind? Surely the essence of God's action in the world consists precisely in working towards this incorporation and universal unity on the mystical level of grace.

And in this great historical awakening of entire continents now taking place before us, can we not also see a symptom indicating this leavening of grace, unifying and so rapidly and effectively creating the history in which we are living?

That is the basis for the great hope we have for the history of to-day and to-morrow; peoples and nations are inwardly, organically, undergoing a development—of grace and nature together—of unification: the lovely prayer of our Redeemer, "that they may be one" (John xvii. 21), is showing itself ever more clearly as the essential law of human history.

Dr. Marga A. M. Klompe was born on 16th August 1912 in Arnhem (Holland). She took her doctorate in science at Utrecht University, and was Professor of Chemistry and Physics at Mater Dei College, Nymwegen, from 1932 to 1949.

From 1947 to 1952, Dr. Marga Klompe was a member of the Dutch Delegation to the UN General Assembly; from 1949 to 1956, member of the Consultative Assembly of the Council of Europe, and from 1952 to 1956, member of the Assembly of the European Coal and Steel Community.

Elected to Parliament in 1948, Marga Klompe remained a Member of the Lower House until October 1956, when she became Minister for Social Welfare in the Netherlands Government.

The Christian's Task in the Formation of a Supranational Community

MARGA KLOMPE

The world in which the Christian is placed is continually changing; and the Christian's task in the world changes correspondingly. This is particularly true in our own century, when we are witnessing great and deep changes in the circumstances of our existence. We have the impression of being in the rapid current of a tremendous evolution, whose direction it is difficult for us to discern, and more difficult still to influence. One of the characteristic features of this evolution is undoubtedly the victory over distance and the rapid intensification of contacts, both in the ordinary and in the deeper sense of the term. Thanks to a technical progress with which we can hardly keep pace, news penetrates from the furthest regions of the world into the smallest and most intimate spheres of each individual existence and of wide sectors of the community; and that with such rapidity and through so many highly developed means of communication that an uninterrupted stream of detailed information reaches us on the happenings of practically the entire world. The joys and sorrows, the problems and desires, the faces and the voices of men and women in Africa and Asia, at times even a voice from those who are suffering and calling for help in the night of Communism ... everything penetrates into the narrow limits of the family circle.

With this victory over distance there is developing also a new vision and a new understanding of the world. Each one of us knows to-day more about the world than the generations which have preceded us. This increased knowledge means greater possibility of direct influence, and therefore also increased responsibility. It is a matter of daily experience that an event taking place to-day in any given part of the globe can have direct consequences, within the shortest space of time, in another, and often distant, part of the world. We are affected by these events, but we are also in a position to influence them without moving from where we are. Our awareness of this fact helps us to realize that the peoples are bound together in a community based on common destiny; that they have, moreover, the concrete, practical possibility of giving visible form to this community, through permanent collaboration, and by creating comprehensive organizations and institutions for a universal community of peoples.

Our century has therefore rightly been called the century of the unification of mankind. We see to-day how states are experiencing almost everywhere the need to join together in wider communities; the South American states are more keenly aware than in past centuries that they must determine together the future of their continent; the Arab peoples are becoming conscious of their common background of language, origin and religion, and are striving to give expression to this common heritage in greater unity; the European peoples are becoming aware of their common cultural, historical and spiritual foundations and are tirelessly seeking new forms of lasting integration.

These limited regional movements towards unification are taking place to-day in all parts of the world and on every continent. A parallel development at a higher level is also taking place toward unification in an all-embracing organization of the community of peoples. Since the Second World War, and on the foundations left by the former League of Nations, the aim has been, and is, to create, in the United Nations, the final community of all peoples throughout the world, based on justice, freedom and peace.

There is no need to stress here the shortcomings, weaknesses and limitations of all these undertakings; we have been made painfully aware of them, moreover, in the very recent past. But these considerations should not make us blind to the fact that the efforts to intensify international collaboration, and this tireless striving to achieve a new structure of international life through supranational activity carried out in a spirit of justice and peace, is something more than mere superficial political opportunism, something more than a clever disguise for ineradicable forms of national egoism. It would be dangerous pessimism not to recognize, in this growth of international collaboration, the positive forces which are at work.

This is largely decisive for the attitude and task of the Christian at the present stage of international development. He must welcome the fact that, in our century, the sense of responsibility towards one's neighbour is not confined within local, regional and national communities, but is becoming a sense of duty towards mankind as such. It is most strongly characteristic of our situation that our neighbour, whom Christ bids us love, is to be found to-day in the whole world; that our international responsibility and solidarity are not felt as a kind of work of supererogation but existentially, as an integral part of our Christian existence in the world, in this world of here and now. We cannot escape this responsibility, and we have to admit that, with our increased knowledge of the needs of under-developed peoples, and the hunger and distress in the overpopulated regions of the Orient, and the cruelty of the persecutions against the Church, our obligations have indeed increased.

This, as we have said, is a new situation, which brings out clearly the grace—and, at the same time, the duty—which the Christian has received from the beginning through his faith: the unity of the human race, established anew, through Christ's work of redemption, which must be brought to ever more visible reality in the world.

The Christian is aware that he will never fully carry out this task. He knows that he is forever putting obstacles in the way of this unity and community of peoples by the inadequacy of the means at his disposal and through his weakness; through mistrust, hatred, envy, jealousy, national egoism and a political opportunism based on purely economic considerations. But he cannot and may not ever grow tired of striving for this aim with all his strength, with the consciousness that by so doing he is carrying out the will of the divine Creator.

It is precisely when the Christian is filled with the idea of this Christ-given unity of mankind that he will seek out ever new ways and means of making this unity a visible reality in the world, of giving it those forms of community which are within our reach. The repeated attempts at international collaboration will then appear to him something more than outward technical forms of organization; he will recognize in them a deeper inward evolution leading towards a great goal, an evolution in conformity with God's plan.

No one can be blind to the dangers and shortcomings of international collaboration to-day. The more one is pledged to work for this collaboration, especially when it is from religious conviction and sense of duty, the more clearly must one recognize and proclaim these dangers. There is, for example, the increasing danger of a depersonalized institutionalization and collectivization of international collaboration and international aid.

In the Middle Ages the Church's situation was completely different from what it is to-day. In a world where the sacred and the profane were integrated, the Church concerned herself also with the profane and protected man in the totality of his personal existence. With the widening of the divorce between sacred and profane, this task she exercised in the temporal field was, however, assumed first by national, and later even by international, bodies. The latter have often a very limited field of activity and are almost always devoid of any philosophical, let alone religious, foundation. Moreover, since these organizations have a task of world-wide dimensions, they are much more exposed than in former days to excessive technicization and collectivization—a danger which is not foreign even to our larger Christian organizations. Under these circumstances, it is much easier to lose sight of the true aim of all such organizations: the *human* community, i.e., the community of persons. What Romano Guardini has been saying recently about "service of our neighbour" is true in exactly the same way of the service of mankind in general: "In the long run, the way of looking at aid determines the way of giving aid. Aid is also exposed to the danger of turning into an impersonal mechanism, an affair of bureaucracy, organization, of professional activity and officialdom. Once the giving of aid comes to be considered in this matter-of-course and routine manner, it can scarcely avoid turning, for practical purposes, into mechanical routine." And he comes to the conclusion: "It is a fact that what we are seeking cannot be achieved simply through practical experience, scientific methods and accuracy in service, but ultimately only through inward dispositions of open-heartedness, generosity, selflessness and spirit of sacrifice, which must have their source elsewhere. If these are not actively present, the very essence of what we call 'aid' is lost. Aid calls indeed for a relation of person to person, for freedom of appeal and response, and its ultimate meaning is to be found in that community whose bonds, established by God, are the necessities of our human existence." (Romano Guardini, *Der Dienst am Nächsten in Gefahr*, Würzburg, Werkbundverlag, 1956, p. 17 et seq.)

The danger of depersonalization is here clearly indicated, and it is one of the Christian's most important tasks to maintain and deepen the personal relationship not only in aid, in the narrower sense, but in every service rendered to the human community. Only in this way can there be a lasting awareness that efforts made to establish a right order in the international community have their source in charity, and that charity has a universal aspect. The more efficient the machinery and the more specialized the organizations, the easier it is for this deeper motive to be stifled. Guardini stresses his warning on this point: "There is a danger that motives will lose their driving force. The awareness of a duty of person to person is growing less." (Ibid., p. 17.)

All our efforts will also be put to a stern test by other extremely difficult problems, of which help for the under-developed regions and collaboration with the young nations of Africa and Asia are certainly not the least.

The economic and technical difficulties need no further explanation; although we are not yet fully informed on all details of the situation in Asia and Africa, available information is sufficient to make us realize that the Western peoples in general, and Christians in particular, have a tremendous obligation to bring rapid and concrete aid; and one conse-quence of such aid may well be that we shall not be able to take the responsibility for further economic and social progress in our own countries as long as we do not effect corresponding improvements among these peoples.

Much more complicated, however, is the problem of intellectual and cultural collaboration with these peoples, whose youthful nationalism is full of deep-rooted mistrust of the white peoples and the former colonial rulers. This fact is of decisive importance for Christianity, for the white peoples are still the main bearers of Christianity, which thus be-comes included in the general attitude of mistrust. The young leaders of these peoples were for the most part edu-cated in the West—at a time when the West no longer recognized in Christianity the true philosophy of life; at the time of rationalism, liberalism, and also of nineteenth-century nationalism. The representatives of the Oriental peoples met here with spiritual currents which were more or less openly opposed to Christianity; they learned by experi-ence the devastation wrought in Christian and even in Catholic minds by extreme nationalism, which for the Christian should be an intolerable scandal. It must be added also that large sectors of these Oriental peoples have risen very rapidly from a state of social humiliation and age-long stagnation and have endeavoured to reach, at a forced tempo, the economic and technical level of the white races.

It is easy to estimate the great dangers to which these peoples are exposed when the civilized West tries to promote this evolution by accelerated economic and technical assistance, while overlooking the essential bases of our concepts of labour, of the machine, of social relations, of hygiene and education—while losing sight, that is, of the spiritual aspects of the assistance rendered.

Here the Christian's task becomes particularly evident. He must once again become fully aware of the nature of the mission assigned to us by Christ. He must recognize once again in the preaching of God's word the fullness of the message of salvation, and must seek to present this message in all its purity, over and above all cultural differences. In this way he will be able, even in temporal matters, to choose the right orientation, in a Christian spirit, and to give new forms to the activity incumbent upon him in the economic, social, technical and educational spheres. An immense field of work opens up here for the layman; as a Christian, he must make this activity spiritually fruitful and render an assistance which is not exclusively material in nature; this spiritual contribution is indispensable if the ultimate aim of all international collaboration is not to be missed.

The question of methods depends upon the various concrete situations. In view of the immense problems involved, it would be an airy illusion to suppose that Catholics can face this task alone and within their own organizations. The mission we have received certainly implies the obligation of collaborating with our ecclesiastical bodies and our Catholic organizations to create living conditions which will be worthy of human beings and therefore most favourable for the reception of Christianity. In doing so, however, we must neither overestimate our own strength nor underestimate the vast dimensions of the problems involved: in the economic and technical fields only a joint effort on the part of all concerned can have any chance of success. Here the Christian's task is to co-operate with all his strength, but with his own spirit and personal convictions, in the realization of existing plans and the work of existing organizations; he must also do all that is in his power to ensure that this joint work of assistance and this great *concours mutuel* of all peoples is in conformity with the divine and natural order, or at least is not contrary to this order, and creates the conditions necessary for the deeper activity implied in the Christian's supernatural task. This co-operation is in the long run a gain for the Christian, since it allows him to concentrate his limited resources on his own essential task and not to drain them in a fruitless endeavour to afford, alone, economic aid to a world of more than a thousand million men.

It is therefore not a matter of either-or, but of a well-balanced both-and, involving differences of method and emphasis.

In this way the Christian will be able to carry out to best advantage his real function in the modern world with its multiple international tasks and organizations; he will be able, that is, to be the herald of a higher aim for this collaboration, a herald of the true, supernatural significance of the community of nations. The importance of this task, precisely in the field of collaboration with the Asian and African peoples, is clear from a report made by the Vice-President of the United States after a journey of several weeks on the African continent; the report stresses the added importance which progress in technology has given to ideas and principles in the struggle for the minds of men.

The Christian's desire to carry out his duty in the international field will, however, be put to a terrible test by the existence of Communism; a test of the individual conscience from which no one can escape. How can we show our readiness to practise charity, effective love and peaceful collaboration when millions of human beings are living under a régime which fights against any coexistence in truth with all the means of coercion and diabolical deception? Is there not here a temptation to dispense oneself from the duty of collaboration, and to resign oneself to giving up all hope of bridging the chasm between West and East? We may, of course, never let ourselves be drawn into any rash compromise, and so become victims of a subtle temptation against which the Holy Father explicitly warned us in his Christmas Message for 1956. But as Christians we may not and cannot give up hope altogether; our mandate is still valid in face of the most absolute refusal from Communism to recognize and respect the true principles of international order. We must, at least, remember to pray that these obstacles will be overcome; we must remain united in prayer with Christians who are suffering and with the Silent Church behind the Iron Curtain; above all, we must be serious about our practice of charity here where we are still free and have the freedom to bear witness to our Christianity.

Only when we make serious efforts to establish a true Christian order in the social and cultural fields on this side of the Iron Curtain can we hope to be taken seriously as Christians on the other side of it; only then can we hope that our witness will have the force to break through all barriers. Have we already done all that could and should be done? No genuine Christian will strive earnestly against Communism without being filled with deep dissatisfaction at all we have left undone, and a firm resolution to do far more in our own part of the world.

On every point, in every field and by all current problems, we are thus obliged each time to formulate our present task in the light of the great international evolution which is taking place, and to reformulate it where corrections are necessary and indispensable.

By way of summary I might express the following wish: the Christian should be present in international work, not only in a physical, but also in a religious and an intellectual sense. If, without being exhaustive, I may make certain recommendations, what I mean in concrete terms is this:

In the religious sphere, we must realize that our way of thinking is too closely linked with our Western civilization and our Western tradition. Christian teaching needs to be studied over again, and seen with the eyes of non-European peoples; their mentality is very different from our own, but has every right to be respected by us in a Christian spirit. The Church's message of salvation is a supernatural one and transcends all differences in culture and tradition. Only when we are aware of this fact shall we be able to translate into deeds our responsibility—even in the temporal sphere—for all our fellow men throughout the world.

In practice, we must also reconsider our traditional ways and means of evangelization, communication and dialogue with others; we must ask ourselves whether, in view of the rapid development of media of communication, and the modernization of man's vision of the world, we do not need to find, in our relations with the masses and with formerly less-developed peoples, more suitable formulations, a modern language, a terminology—in the deeper sense—better adapted to other peoples. I am thinking, for instance, of new liturgical forms adapted to the young nations with their very different conceptions, and the strongly contemplative orientation of their spiritual life. The rules of the religious Orders—which have grown up in the West and under different circumstances—should also be adapted, without sacrificing their deeper significance, to the needs of peoples of different mentality.

In the intellectual sphere two things seem to be needed:

In the first place, international Catholic Institutes should rapidly be set up for the study of the various international problems and fields of activity; here ecclesiastics and competent laypeople would carry out together a careful scientific study of all aspects of a given problem, on the basis of exact analysis of the present situation, which is often known only in a fragmentary fashion (I am thinking of the various countries, continents, peoples, ethnic groups, etc., where Christianity is in special danger or has still to be preached, of the masses estranged from the Church, of the population problem, of Communism, of modern atheism in all its forms, of the youth problem, of organized forms of charitable activity, etc.). It goes without saying to-day that, before any concrete planning can be taken into consideration, there must first be a systematic development of the under-developed territories, including part of South America. This all means that such institutes must be organized on the spot, and therefore on a decentralized basis and independently of ecclesiastical geography. There are already several encouraging attempts in this sense, but the whole thing needs to be developed systematically.

In the second place, the Christian's presence in all international organisms, organizations and institutions is a commandment for the present day. But we must ask ourselves whether our lay forces are already adequate to these great international tasks, or whether some very intensive work has not to be done for the training of national and regional personnel, and that for some years before they can be launched into action? To ask a question means to give an answer, and in this case an affirmative answer. Our "presence" can only be achieved if Christians are disposed to prepare for it by scientific training, thorough competence and tireless energy, and above all if they are animated by a just appreciation of the great value of such activity as part of the work to be undertaken, under Christ's banner, for the salvation and redemption of mankind.

This brings us back to our starting point. The Christian who has a right understanding of his task in international collaboration to-day is constantly aware that he is only an instrument, a servant, of the divine Master. He knows that, even with the greatest competence and the utmost zeal, he can accomplish nothing without the help of the Spirit who alone can change the face of the earth. And so, over and over again, he must draw from the wellspring of religious inspiration; in working for international collaboration, international aid and the pacification and ordering of the community of nations, he must bring into play the strength derived from a deep, personal and existential experience of the life of charity, which is the source of his personal commitment. Only in this way will he rightly carry out and rightly understand the service which, as a Christian, he must render to mankind. Only in this way will all his efforts to bring about a peaceful community of peoples become in the true sense an apostolate and, with God's help, a fruitful apostolate, at the service of the unity of the human race, for whose redemption Christ offered himself in sacrifice.

Raymond Scheyven was born in Brussels on 26th November 1911. After studying the humanities at the Institut Saint-Louis, he took his Doctorate of Law at Louvain University in 1932, and practised as a barrister at the Court of Appeal in Brussels.

General Secretary of the Belgian Savings Bank from 1935-6, he was from 1936 to 1952 Manager of the Jos Allard Bank and administrator of various financial concerns.

A member of the Belgian Delegation to the UN in 1946-7, Raymond Scheyven was a delegate to the Economic and Social Council of the UN in 1952; Chairman of ECOSOC in 1953, he was entrusted by the UN General Assembly with a special mission for financial assistance to under-developed countries (1954-5).

His numerous other responsibilities include: Member of Parliament for Brussels since 1946; Municipal Councillor since 1952; President of the Christian Social Party for Brussels City; member of the Party's National Committee, and National Treasurer; member of the Finance Commission of the House of Representatives for Foreign Affairs, Foreign Trade and Structural Reform; reporter to the House on bills concerning Benelux, the Marshall Plan, NATO, the budget for roads and transport, the budget of the Foreign Office, etc.; Chairman of the Economic and Social Committee of the Nouvelles Equipes Internationales (Union of Christian Democrats).

During the Resistance, Raymond Scheyven was head of the "Socrates" Secret Service and responsible for financial aid to resistants.

His decorations include a Military Cross, Grand Officer of the Order of Leopold for activities in the Resistance, the Silver Star, and O.B.E.

Help for Economically Underdeveloped Countries

RAYMOND SCHEYVEN

THE VICTORY OF WANT

The wealthy nations are still too ignorant of the want prevailing in the world, despite the fact that during these last years men of high intellectual stature and moral worth have made their voices heard in describing the proportions which it has assumed. Their contribution has been a most valuable one and the descriptive study of this distress may now be said to be complete; it opens our eyes to a dramatic situation, for it shows that to eat one's fill and to live decently are still to-day privileges reserved for a minority of human beings.

These facts and the consequences deriving from them must penetrate into the minds of men; public opinion in every country—in a special way, Catholic circles—must become aware that one of the major tasks of our day is still the struggle against dire poverty. The problem is, however, so vast that one cannot expect to deal with it comprehensively in a few pages. We must limit ourselves to a bare outline, stressing the more significant facts.

It is hard to imagine, without having seen it, the real nature of this dire poverty which oppresses the greater part of the human race. In Africa, Asia, Latin America and the Near and Middle East, hundreds of millions of human beings are inexorably doomed, through poverty, to endure hunger and to live in unhealthy hovels. Endemic diseases find in them an easy prey. Hundreds of millions of human beings are illiterate and their ignorance lends an air of fatalism to their distress. Even in Europe, vast territories are still zones of poverty, disease and ignorance.

Hunger leads the procession of miseries. Not just the occasional hunger due to some exceptional penury, but the daily, endemic hunger known to more than one and a half milliard human beings,[1] i.e., to nearly two-thirds of the human race. In their civilized comfort and their faith in progress, some might think that this state of affairs is on the way to improvement. Unfortunately, this is not the case—quite the contrary: the percentage of the world's population which is definitely undernourished has risen from 38.6 per cent before the war to 59.5 per cent at the present time.[2] It is almost unbelievable that in spite of the tremendous power of the means at our disposal, at a time of unprecedented scientific and technical progress, we have not been able to solve the world's food problem.

It is in this perspective that the world's population is increasing at the rate of 80,000 human beings daily,[3] i.e., approximately 30 millions annually. Unless adequate steps are taken, the problem will only increase; according to a United Nations study, the world's population, which was 2 milliard 400 million in 1950, could reach the figure of 3 milliard 600 million in about thirty years.[4]

As was seen by the United Nations General Assembly, the problem of hunger goes together with that of slums. A large part of the human race is living in promiscuity. Innumerable families live cooped up in one room, and for the most part in small, dark, unhealthy mud huts. Such housing conditions preclude the most elementary hygiene and are a factor in the spread of infectious diseases.[5]

These conditions as regards nutrition and housing weaken the whole organism and make it an easy prey for disease. And

[1] See *Population*, Paris, Institut national d'études démographiques, Oct.-Dec. 1953, p. 631.
[2] See *Preliminary Report on the World Social Situation*, U.N. Publications, Sales No. 1952. IV. 11, p. 41, table VII.
[3] See "The Past and Future Growth of World Population", U.N. Publications, Sales No. 1952. XIII. 2, *Population Bulletin*, no. 1, Dec. 1951, p. 8.
[4] See *The Determinants and Consequences of Population Trends*, U.N. Publications, Sales No. 1953. XIII. 3, p. 161.
[5] See *Preliminary Report*, p. 58.

so cholera, pneumonia, malaria, tuberculosis, trachoma, etc., are rife in vast sectors of the globe. The enquiries made by the World Health Organization[1] show that some 300 million human beings are suffering from malaria. In the urban agglomerations of the underdeveloped areas there are four times as many victims of tuberculosis as in the cities of Western countries. In the Near East, the Middle East and South-East Asia, trachoma is rife, and other ophthalmic diseases leading to blindness. Epidemics of cholera, typhoid fever and yellow fever still devastate parts of the globe at regular intervals, while gastric diseases, due to poverty and malnutrition, take a heavy toll.

The physical and intellectual vitality of many populations is thus undermined from infancy; whence an irremediable weakening of their capacity for work and their physical and moral resistance. And so hundreds of millions of human beings succumb prematurely to exhaustion after an unequal battle waged from birth against hunger, disease and despair, a battle which their fathers and mothers have waged and lost already before them.

In the educational field, the picture is just as depressing: half of the adults in the world can neither read nor write and, in the underdeveloped countries, persons with any intellectual formation number less than 4 per cent of the total population. In some countries illiterates are more than 80 per cent.[2]

We are confronted in this way with a vicious circle which is really tragic: poverty, malnutrition and disease undermine the vitality of these populations and lessen their capacity for the tremendous effort required for their uplift. If this situation was prolonged, it would lead to grave social and political problems and would end by making the most desperate solutions attractive to these populations. The threat of dire poverty is one to which the industrialized countries may not remain blind.

[1] Ibid. p. 24.
[2] See *Annuaire statistique 1949-50*, U.N. publications, 1950, XVIII. 3.

FULFILLING OUR DUTY AS CHRISTIANS

I feel it is superfluous to prove that dire poverty is an evil and that no one may remain indifferent at the sight of it.

We all have the duty to fight against distress and despair. And yet, I sometimes meet people who cannot be moved by a description and the statistics of hunger and disease. These people do not understand that the situation of the under-developed countries is morally intolerable and that all indifference and passivity in this regard are blameworthy in conscience. They assert that the outcasts of this world are not as wretched as we think; that, like their forebears, they have never known better living conditions and do not suffer as we would suffer ourselves. This is not the place for long theories on the relativity of happiness. Suffice it to say that these poor people are human beings like ourselves and that we, especially we Christians, have therefore the imperative duty of enabling them to live as men with a God-given destiny. Human beings may not be divided into two categories, a first category, comprising a third of the human race, to which we belong and which has the right to decent living, and a second category—the other two-thirds of mankind—which is obliged to live in material circumstances often worse than those reserved among us for domestic animals.

The problem raised is, in short, that of the responsibility of Western civilization, of "Christian civilization". Many, almost all, underdeveloped countries are, we have to admit, ex-colonies, where we had undertaken to carry out what we have so often called "a great work of civilization". Have we really proved worthy of this task of civilization, which was the only justification for our presence?

I have often wondered, when passing through certain of these countries, what prodigies of eloquence I should have needed to win the assent of these millions of men and women for the great political party to which all or nearly all of us belong in our own countries, the party which defends human rights and affirms the sacred character of the human person. What, indeed, could I have said to these men and women who have never known freedom and for whom the civilization we wish to see triumph, far from establishing living conditions compatible with the respect due to their person, has so far brought only famine, disease, ignorance and despair? Is it not tragic that we are obliged to ask this question? But would it not be a still greater tragedy to leave it without reply precisely when all the elements for a solution are in our hands? Time is short; to-morrow the population of the underdeveloped countries will have increased by millions of human beings whose presence will make it much more difficult to solve our problem. To-morrow, too, the challenge from the Communist world will be still more formidable; when its positions have been consolidated, its dominion firmly established over the satellite powers, when it has China marching by its side, the fascination it exerts could become invincible. To-day, the resources of the free world are greater than those of the Communist world, but let us be watchful; for industrial and technical progress is making giant strides on the other side of the Iron Curtain. Soon we may be overtaken, and even outstripped, and then it will be too late: irresistibly, the needy peoples will be seduced and enslaved.

THE UNDERDEVELOPED COUNTRIES
AND THE TEMPTATION OF COMMUNISM

At first sight, this fascination of Communism seems inexplicable enough. Nevertheless, it is a reality; we can see the beginnings of revolutionary movements in almost all parts of Asia and Africa, wherever want has prepared the way for Communism. It is clearly not the police régime nor the so-called dictatorship of the proletariat nor the "re-education camps" that fascinate the underdeveloped peoples: it would seem to be Communism's efficiency which constitutes for them a terrible temptation.

This efficiency is assured by dictatorship, whether of a man or of the Party. We may, we should, not like this fact; we have to admit, however, that if democracy and a parliamentary régime can function satisfactorily in highly-developed countries like our own, they prove ineffective in other countries, and more especially in underdeveloped regions where only an authoritarian régime can "succeed". Let us, then, be clear-sighted and courageous enough to admit that, precisely because it brings with it a political dictatorship, Communism has a better chance of success than the democracies we should try to establish.

Should we not also admit the possibility of several different régimes in the economic field? May I say that I am by no means convinced of the universal excellence of the capitalist régime, based essentially on private initiative, the profit motive and freedom of competition. One may wonder, indeed, whether an economic system of this kind is likely to succeed in less advanced countries which lack precisely these three driving forces.

The Communist régime is based, for its part, on the collectivization of all the means of production. What is more, if I have rightly understood what goes on in the U.S.S.R., the person responsible for an agricultural district or an industrial concern has to answer for the success of the undertaking entrusted to him. The stake is his wellbeing, his freedom and, at times, even his life. Soviet workers have to be "on the dot" at factory or office, under pain of forfeiting a considerable part of their salary, even of their freedom. We revolt, and rightly, against such methods; we cannot imagine the necessity of threatening our industrial leaders with imprisonment. They have—thanks be to God—enough spirit of initiative and profit-making sense; and there is the urge of competition, the urge to outdo one's neighbours. We do not think, either, of compelling our workmen or employees to be punctual by force. But can the same qualities be demanded from moujiks who lack the traditional zeal of our workers and contractors, from men and women—so frequently met with in the underdeveloped countries—who have never learned to work, in the pitiless heat of the sun; men and women who, after centuries of dire poverty, have scarcely any needs to satisfy?

Communism does not, of course, give a valid answer to these questions. The indolence of the moujik is clearly no justification for a philosophy which places society at the summit of its scale of values and implacably subordinates man to the good of the collectivity. Communists do not have that respect for the human person which is the very basis of our Christian philosophy. For them, the individual does not count, or counts for little. Once this thesis has been accepted, everything becomes clear in the Communist régime. In accordance with teachings inculcated in him by the Party from his earliest infancy, the militant must denounce "without any consideration for persons", whoever is not a good servant of society.[1]

The same justification is good in Communist eyes for arrests, the transplantation of entire populations, forced labour, concentration camps and even "spontaneous confessions". A militant, when arrested, must confess his errors publicly, if such a confession is deemed useful for society, if it is likely to rekindle the flame of enthusiasm in members of the Party.

We Christians have too great a respect for the human person to accept this philosophy. The inhuman consequences of Communism's inhuman philosophy cannot be too plainly denounced. But do not let us be duped by words and satisfied with theoretical anti-Communism. To the shortsighted, the Communist could easily reply that society is, after all, only the totality of the persons composing it and that to work for the good of society is therefore to ensure the happiness of the individuals who make up society. Is it not legitimate, he could say, to sacrifice a few million human

[1] Mr. Malenkov's report to the Nineteenth Congress of the Party: "If things are going badly in one or another organization and the interests of the Party and the State are suffering, the Party member has the obligation, over and above all consideration of persons, to make the deficiencies known to the governing bodies, including the Central Committee. This is the duty of every Communist, and the primary duty of a Party member."

beings—those imprisoned, subjected to forced labour, confined in "re-education camps"—as the necessary price of ensuring the happiness of tens and hundreds of millions of other human beings? We Christians may not even ask this question, for we know that every human being is created in the likeness of God, destined for a divine dignity, and may not be sacrificed to the happiness of other human beings. Does this mean that we may be content with living a quiet life? It is certainly not by letting our respect for the person degenerate into mere individualism or by developing our personality cult to the point of contempt for the community that we shall prepare to answer the appeal from the needy peoples. A fruitful anxiety should take possession of our souls when we learn, for instance, that Stalin's Constitution, in proclaiming: "If any man will not work, neither let him eat", is only taking its text from St Paul's Second Epistle to the Thessalonians (iii. 10).

The revolutionary principle on which Communists base their doctrine and their methods proves also terribly efficient. Wherever they take control, they get rid of the men in power, liquidate the ruling classes and imprison the "feudal lords". It must be admitted that this brutal entrance staged for the revolution is far more efficient than our serene respect for the past. We have learned, unfortunately, that in many underdeveloped countries, it would not be much use sending technicians and investing capital if, at the same time, certain reforms were not effected and power taken out of certain incompetent and corrupt hands. Where the Communists effect a revolution, we have at heart the respect of established order, or more exactly, disorder.

This thought was uppermost in my mind recently when I was speaking with a diplomat, representing a great Asian republic, who pointed to indispensable reforms urgently needed in his country, such as an agrarian reform which would make available to the population at large lands which to-day remain unexploited and are the property of a few great landowners. Although this diplomat was by no means a Communist and himself belonged to this class of great landed proprietors, he added, at the close of our conversation, that this was the reason which led so many young people in his country to look towards Moscow and Communism; they felt the need for a revolution, no other expedient seeming likely in their eyes to free their homeland from its millenial stagnation.

So it is that, in their struggle for world conquest, involving to-day a little more than half of the human race, the Communists would seem to have at their disposal weapons more effective than our own. And yet, what miracles free economy can effect when its existence is in danger, as, for instance, in time of war. And need we recall the admirable—and wholly pacific—work carried out by the United States under the Marshall Plan in the countries of Western Europe? In four years, the United States of America administered aid in our countries to the extent of 13 milliard 500 million dollars, 90 per cent in the form of gifts and 10 per cent in loans at an interest of from 2.5 to 4 per cent. The burden of taxation imposed on the American people averaged, for the first year, 40 dollars per head, and 100 dollars per tax-payer. Certain countries were literally "snatched away" from Communism thanks to the economic aid generously given by the United States.

But to-day, it is not only a matter of the countries of Western Europe; the world's fate is being decided in Asia, in Africa, in Latin America. Our rulers, employers and unions are certainly worthy of high praise in their efforts constantly to improve the living standard of our populations. But let us not forget the lesson of history: revolutions come to birth whenever the difference between rich and poor becomes too great in any given country. But, in our day, there are scarcely any frontiers left between countries, or between continents. True, poverty and want have been the lot of the greater part of the human race throughout the centuries; but to-day a new factor has appeared: needy populations everywhere are beginning to realize that their situation can be improved through modern techniques, and they aspire to greater wellbeing. It is the duty of our civilization to satisfy these legitimate aspirations, if it is not to disappear.

The years we are living through—the very months—are those of our last chance!

Kotaro Tanaka was born in 1890 at Kagoshima, Kyushu (Japan). He graduated in 1915 from Tokyo Imperial University (School of Law), where he was appointed, in 1917, Assistant Professor, and specialized in Commercial Law.

After being sent by the Government to study Commercial Law in the United States, France and Italy from 1919 to 1922, he was appointed Professor at Tokyo Imperial University and continued in service until 1946. From 1937 to 1939 he was Dean of the Faculty of Law, and for more than fifteen years member of the Jury of State Examinations for judges, lawyers and administrative officials. In 1945 he was appointed Chief of School Administration in the Ministry of Education; in 1946, Member of the House of Peers (Upper House), and later Member of the House of Councillors (Upper House). From May 1946 to January 1947, he was Minister of Education in the Yoshida Cabinet. During these years, he was engaged in the practice of law, especially concerning commercial affairs, and he collaborated with government legislation in this field.

In March 1950, Kotaro Tanaka was appointed Chief Justice of the Supreme Court of Japan.

In 1936, he had been invited to Italy as Exchange Professor by the Institute for the Middle and Far East, and had given lectures on Commercial Law and the Philosophy of Law in Rome, Milan, Venice, Paris, Lyons, Lille and Louvain. Later, on the invitation of cultural associations and universities, he lectured also in various university centres of Brazil, Argentina and other countries of Latin America.

Doctor of Law since 1929, Kotaro Tanaka was made in 1941 a Member of the Imperial Academy of Japan, and in 1948 Professor Emeritus of Tokyo University. Among other academic titles, he is Doctor honoris causa *of the Catholic University of Chile, of Fordham and Georgetown Universities, and of Boston College. He is President or Member of various cultural and legal associations.*

His numerous published works deal largely with problems of commercial law, the philosophy of law, and education, but include also travel memoirs, a History of Latin America *and a volume entitled* Catholicism and the Present Day.

A convert to Catholicism, Kotaro Tanaka took the name of Paul at his baptism. He is President of Men's Catholic Action in Tokyo.

His decorations include, together with high state awards from Italy and Spain, the Great Cross of the Order of St. Sylvester, received from the Holy See in 1953.

World Peace and World Law

KOTARO TANAKA

Peace is one of the ideals for which mankind has been struggling for some thousands of years and which it has still never perfectly realized. The fact that we have never reached this goal does not mean that it is unattainable. Who will assert that the ideal of to-day may not be the reality of to-morrow?

For those who, during their lifetimes, have experienced two world wars, yet cannot predict that the last war will be final, for those witnessing ever-increasing violent competition in heavy armaments among the Powers, it is only natural that peace should appear no more than a pious dream, and they necessarily become pessimistic concerning the prospects of the world-society.

But those who do not agree with the fatalistic view of human history and its eschatology, and believe in man's lofty mission of active participation in the historical process of realizing the ideal conceived by the Creator, will not be so easily discouraged by the successive failures of efforts for peace and by the cruel realities of human society. On the contrary, when they carefully trace the historical evolution of thousands of years, they will delight in reckoning up the achievements of the civilization and culture attained by our forefathers, and they will be ever conscious of their heavy but glorious responsibility of following the same path and enriching the heritage handed down to our own generation.

In our efforts aiming at peace, we must not be too impatient. If we consider that the history of the political life of mankind is immeasurably short compared with the long space of time since the first creation of man, that the reform of political life is far more difficult than the conversion of an individual and that, in spite of these facts, enormous progress has been made during the last half-century in the effort to realize peace, we shall not be pessimistic about our progress towards it.

The problem of peace may be approached from several sides. It is hard to find a more complicated problem; legal, moral, political, economic and religious paths run together at the crossroads of peace. In considering this problem we must be on guard against the danger of emphasizing one aspect and ignoring the others. The predominance of one method, the utmost exclusivism in considering a matter of such complexity, is one of the weaknesses of contemporary social science, traceable to the tendency to extreme specialization in academic activities.

What is required of us is a consciousness of the fact that the problem of peace is deeply rooted in human nature, and its solution therefore dependent upon the conception we possess of that nature. Religious sentimentalism which shows complete disregard of social facts does not suffice to a complete solution, just as the thoroughly-planned regimentation of world economy itself does not guarantee perpetual peace.

Briefly, there is no other way of attacking this problem than the application of the methods required in social science generally—speculative and empiric, theoretical and historical, spiritual and realistic, idealistic and positivistic, and so on. We cannot agree with any so-called monism where method is concerned. Man, with his flesh and instincts, which belong to the realm of nature, as a rational being belongs to the world of the spirit, and the noble mission of the human being is nothing other than the spiritualization of nature. The peace so eagerly desired is inseparably connected with this mission, in that peace means the termination of the state in which men are as wolves toward one another, and each wages war upon all the rest. There is no peace in the jungle. The human being alone has the privilege of striving for peace.

The concept of peace derives directly from that of the social nature of man which was first clearly articulated by Aristotle. This nature, by reason of the consanguinity of all peoples, has a scope which is unlimited and embraces the whole world. Jacques Maritain pointed out that a "person" is "an open whole" (*un tout ouvert*). Man needs his fellow-men, not just because he is different from other creatures in his bodily, intellectual and moral life; this characteristic finds its origin also in the fundamental generosity imprinted in the existence of the person itself—in that openness to the communication of knowledge and of love which are inherent in the spirit. The object of this openness is unlimited in extent; in proportion to the expansion of the sphere of human intercourse, the circle affected by this openness goes beyond family, tribe, city and state, and may potentially embrace the whole of humanity. A world-society and world-economy have come to have real existence; the world-community is no more an idle dream.

The question is what kind of relations should exist between men and groups belonging to the world-community. And there is no doubt that above all peace must govern this community.

What is the meaning of peace? As far as I am concerned here, I mean, not peace in the religious sense (for instance, *Et in terra pax hominibus bonae voluntatis*, or the *pax* of St. Augustine), but that state of human society in which the predominance of violence ceases and anarchy comes to an end. Peace is the antithesis of the state of anarchy and the rule of violence.

However, the simple absence of anarchy and violence does not mean peace. The peace of the South Pole is not in the real sense peace, nor is a peace established by the oppression of a dictator—we can conceive as the ultimate possibility that the overwhelming violence of one single man might come to replace the multitude of individual violences, but human dignity and freedom would then be out of the question.

Anarchy as the negation of peace and despotism as enforced peace are essentially the same in nature, being products of a political society which is not adequately trained in democratic discipline, as some phases of the history of the Latin American republics after their attainment of independence sufficiently demonstrate.

The peace worth pursuing is intimately related to justice. Without justice, there is no true peace. As justice is fundamentally identical with law, law is one of the most important factors in peace. Furthermore, it is not an exaggeration to say that peace means the rule of law and that peace is identical with law.

In emphasizing the meaning of law for peace, we have to be wary of falling into the error of believing in the omnipotence of law, as did the legists represented in ancient China by Han Fei-Tse, and the Western positivist school from Macchiavelli and Hobbes to the second half of the nineteenth century. It is superfluous to emphasize that law is organically interrelated with morality, that the perfect observance of legal precepts in its final instance depends upon the moral conscience of individuals, and that the norms of law embody many ethical concepts prevailing in society. We cannot ignore the truth that realization of the ideal of peace, one of the loftiest aspirations of mankind, cannot be attained by means of law alone, without any help from religion, morality and other elements in culture. But at the same time it is undeniable that the proportionate importance of the parts played by law, religion and morals in the peaceful establishment of social life varies in accordance with the nature and extent of the human groups concerned. In family life we are hardly conscious of the necessity of family law; here the predominance of morality and custom is striking. In commercial society the importance of the legal precepts increases in degree; still, there are differences between small societies (such as partnerships) and large ones (such as private corporations). If we think of religious organizations like the Catholic Church, we can see that in contradiction to the superficial concept of antagonism between law and religion represented by Rudolf Sohm, the factor of law assumes added importance for the purpose of guaranteeing the objectivity of faith, as well as of maintaining the extensive hierarchical structure of the Church. It is needless to mention the important role played by it in the State. So it is quite natural that in Western countries the preponderance of the role of law in the realization of peace in world society is generally recognized, not only among jurists proper but among all those deeply concerned with the problem of peace. Concretely speaking, the core of the study of this problem is found in such questions as how anarchy among nations can be overcome, how the sanction of international law and the effectiveness of treaties may be guaranteed, in what direction the future organization of international society should proceed, what should be the sovereignty of each national state in the international organization, and the like.

Briefly, the problem of peace, in the sense of the establishment of a new legal order among conflicting sovereign states, as opposed to appealing to the armed force of each state, is essentially of a legal nature. This problem can be reduced to that of the realization of the rule of law in international society, or more concretely the establishment of world law (or universal law), the creation of an effective world organization and international legislative policy toward peace.

The concept of World Law, first proposed in 1888 in the work *Möglichkeit eines Weltrechts* by a German scholar, Ernst Zitelman, Professor of Civil Law at the University of Bonn, and developed by his followers, including Peter Klein, was concerned with some areas of private law, especially with the law of contract and commercial transactions, which are susceptible of being unified among different civilized nations. In my own work, *A Theory of World Law*, first published in Japan in 1933-5, I tried to extend this idea to the two other branches of law, that is, private international law (the conflict of laws) and public international law (the law of nations), which can be said to be laws of the world-society at large. The former is concerned with regulation of intercourse among individuals belonging to different nations; the latter is the law by which the relations of sovereign national units are regulated. My idea is that some fundamental concepts of law transcending national frontiers are necessarily to be found as common denominator for the basis of these two fields of law. What I tried to do was to find a synthesis of several branches of law affecting the international life of individuals as well as of nations, and a systematization of laws relating to international life upon the basis of the concepts of a world society and of natural law. Now that we are confronting the radical change in international life brought about by the recent stupendous progress in international communications and intercourse, by radio and aeronautics, and an ever-increasing and intensifying political, military, economic and cultural interdependence and solidarity among nations, a Copernican revolution in the field of legal concepts has become particularly urgent. The traditional views—that the law is the will of the sovereign State (the school of Austin) or the natural manifestation of national characteristics (the German historical school)—not only may be criticized theoretically, but have proved themselves completely inadequate to meet the needs of the present circumstances of international life. The legal science of the present day still, unfortunately, remains in a state of stagnation. Generally speaking, the famous criticism pronounced more than half a century ago by Rudolf Ihering, in his *Geist des römischen Rechts*, still prevails in the contemporary science of law: "The science of the thing is reduced to national jurisprudence ... a humiliating and unworthy form for a science to take." World peace is very enthusiastically desired, but we find very few who give consideration to the legal foundation of peace.

To my great satisfaction, I have found a very remarkable defender of universal law in the person of Mr. Emery Reves, whose book *The Anatomy of Peace* (1945), although not extensive in itself, has attracted great public interest, and even in my own country has exerted great influence in promoting the World Federal State Movement. The author puts forward an analysis of failures or fallacies in capitalism, socialism and religion, all of which, in his view, inevitably lead to war or to antagonism, and are inadequate to solve the problem of peace; and he declares that war is inevitable between groups of men forming social units (tribes, dynasties, churches, cities, nations) when these units exercise unrestricted sovereign power. And he insists that the only way of suppressing war is to be found in transferring the sovereign power of these social units to larger or higher units. According to Mr. Reves, all attempts made in the past to maintain peace, all ideas proposed for this purpose—including the League of Nations, the Kellogg-Briand Pact, the idea of collective security, the principles of independence and self-determination, balance of power and regionalism, the Atlantic Charter, the United Nations Declaration, etc.—are, since they are based on the recognition of sovereign nation states, not only ineffective—"nothing more than a pious expression of vague and unreal hope"—but simply accelerate the tempo of war. In short, he denies radically the concept of internationalism, because it presupposes the co-existence of sovereign nation states, which inevitably leads to conflict and war. The only solution, as he untiringly repeats, is to be found in the establishment of world government, in "the integration of the scattered conflicting national sovereignties into one unified higher sovereignty, capable of creating a legal order within which all peoples may enjoy equal security, equal obligations and equal rights under law."

Personally, as one who has dedicated more than half of his academic career to the study of world law in connection with the problem of peace, I cannot help admiring the far-sightedness of his views and his rational and logical way of thinking. We have been very clearly shown the goal to which

the evolution of human society is to be orientated, and profoundly encouraged and stimulated in pursuing this lofty
ideal.

I should like, however, to make some comments upon a
few points in his argument.

His criticism of the absolute sovereignty of nation states as
the cause of conflict, war and international anarchy is in itself perfectly just; nevertheless we have to recall the fact that,
theoretically, the dogma of absolute sovereignty was completely overthrown by the representatives of the pluralistic
conception of the State, including Hobhouse, Duguit and
Krabbe, as well as by internationalists (for instance, by
Jitta). Almost all of the scholars who have urged the legal
nature of international law, criticizing the theory of "self-
limitation" (*Selbstverpflichtung*) insisted upon by Jellinek, have
reached the conclusion of recognizing the existence of some
objective super-state norms prevailing in international
society, no matter whether they belong to the category of
positive law or to that of natural law, and without regard to
whether they are guaranteed by a coercive sanction. This
way of reasoning, as we all know, has been most clearly and
energetically represented by the thinkers of the more academic type. But the real problem is the practical question of
how the effectiveness of international law can be guaranteed;
above all, how for this purpose the world organization to
which the sovereign powers of all nation states are to be
transferred may without serious disturbances be established.
To draft a constitution for a World Government and to
elaborate at one's desk a system of world law, is the work of
but a few days. Indeed, we all know that already many
excellent plans for world organization have been published.
But the creation of a world organization will not be realized
so long as the causes of conflicts of political and economic
interests between nations exist and clashes between them
remain inevitable. The establishment of World Government
must go side by side with the growth of innumerable international institutions with the purpose of regulating specific

conflicting material interests of all kinds between nations. To use the scholastic terminology, we cannot realize the *iustitia generalis* (or *legalis*) without establishing the *iustitia distributiva* and *iustitia commutativa*. The maintenance of the *iustitia generalis*, that is, the realization of peace in a given society, belongs to the mission of a government. But if at the same time the *iustitia distributiva* and *iustitia commutativa* between members of the society are not realized, peace will assuredly be in peril. Otherwise, even if a World Government existed, it would remain only nominal, and the concepts of "civil war" and international police action would be nothing but a transparent camouflage for naked international war and employment of military power.

I do not doubt the desirability of the renunciation of sovereignty by nation states, but I am sceptical of its possibility, so long as this measure does not go *pari passu* with the more perfect realization of the basic material conditions which constitute justice in international society. The creation of World Government may be considered the result of the realization of justice generally, and not *vice versa*.

However, Mr. Reves' proposal is, as we have seen above, diametrically opposed to this point of view. He is unwilling to recognize any effort, any plan for international organization, as being a "first step", but condemns all such as a "continuation of error" and "negative steps", for the reason that they are based on the false principle of *inter*-nationalism. He is inimical to the attitude of the "perfectionists".

Here we are confronted with the alternative: evolution or revolution. What he requires is indeed a Copernican revolution in the international society; but we have to remember that no revolution can be accomplished without the aid of an effective source of internal or external physical force, accompanied by the enormous sacrifice of bloodshed. The saying "Natura non saltat" may properly be applied to solve the international problem. If we do not lose sight of our ideal, and simultaneously do not spare our efforts to solve the traditional and the new individual vital problems of an

international society—more concretely, if we value properly
the organization of the United Nations and UNESCO,
which may be considered, by comparison with the League of
Nations, a big "first step" toward our goal, and try to
strengthen their weaknesses and supply what is lacking in
them—briefly, if we urge on the great current of world
history, we may be quite optimistic that some day our ideal
will become reality.

If we consider the problem of international organization
from the legal point of view only, the historical development
proves that international society is very slowly orientating
itself towards being an organic entity, gradually overcoming
the state of anarchy attributable to the unco-ordinated co-
existence and the rivalry of independent sovereign states.
That this historical fact has exercised its influence upon legal
thinking is evident enough from what we have seen above.
The doctrine of the absolute sovereignty of the State has
gone out of vogue. Furthermore, we have to note the fact that
treaties do not remain a matter of bilateral agreement, but
have come more and more to be a "polylateral" and collective one. Even peace treaties, as with those of Versailles and
San Francisco, are taking the same direction. The legally-
independent individual treaties have become *de facto* consolidated with one another, increasing their coercive force and
being institutionalized. The uniformity of the contents of
treaties tends to create universal institutions.

The evolution of legal form was ingeniously demonstrated
by Sir Henry Maine's "from status to contract". But the line
of legal evolution continues farther, and by the appearance
of a new category of *contrat d'adhésion* the contract develops
towards the category of the "institution" (Maurice Henrion).
As Sgr. Guido Gonella pointed out, in his *Presupposti di un
ordine internazionale* (2d. ed., 1943), the *do-ut-des* principle of
contractualism ought to be integrated with the *solidarietà
istituzionale*, and what is advocated by Mr. Reves may doubt-
less be not far removed from this idea. And the theory and

the facts of international society are following the same line.

Thus in the field of international law, as in that of national law, the principle of individualism will be superseded by that of solidarity.

In scrutinizing the problem of international organization, there is one factor which cannot be entirely overlooked. That involves the question: Is there the possibility of the co-existence of groups subscribing to utterly antagonistic political ideals and the economic systems closely connected therewith (democracy, Fascism, Communism, capitalism)? The answer given by Mr. Reves is affirmative and optimistic. He says, "The only way they [different economic concepts and systems] can coexist peacefully is within one legal system", and continues: "The widespread belief that any unified legal order between the Soviet Union and the Western democracies is impossible because of the fundamental differences in their economic systems, is no more valid than the century-old prejudice that Catholics and Protestants could not live peacefully in the same community".

Here we are obliged to face a problem most fundamental to the consideration of peace, a problem which by its nature belongs to the sphere of ethics and philosophy rather than of law, sociology or economics. Its solution is intimately related to the fundamental concept of peace, and this again is closely united with our ideal of human society, which it is impossible to conceive apart from the meaning and aim of life. This is because it is impossible to conceive of politics, domestic as well as international, as a means of serving mankind, independently of our conception of the mission of human life.

Here necessarily we have to go back to the relation between peace and justice. Peace is a legal order, which is destined to overcome the rule of violence and the state of anarchy among men, and permits of their peaceful co-existence. We have, however, to consider what is the content of peace. If its content is contrary to justice, peace may have no merit. We cannot deny the necessity of struggling for the cause of justice even at the sacrifice of nominal peace; we have to remember that sometimes in our life it is better to shed blood than tears. Peace and justice are correlative concepts.

So we shall not be satisfied with the establishment of world organization and world law in the formal sense. Rather we are concerned with the content of both institutions, with whether they may realize democracy and human rights and contribute to the commonweal, or destroy these values.

The world community, which organization we have been studying as an essential condition of peace, requires at least the political homogeneity implied by a common denominator of certain fundamental political principles; which does not, of course, exclude the heterogeneity of ethnic, religious, economic and cultural elements, as the United States of America, Switzerland and Brazil excellently illustrate. In a federal state the autonomy of each member state cannot be permitted to go so far as to recognize the institution of slavery. We cannot imagine any coexistence of "two worlds" when in the one truth is distorted, man is enslaved, people are deprived of important fundamental rights and freedoms, secret trials are held and children spy on their parents; and in the other human rights and freedoms not only are guaranteed by the letter of the law, but are protected in actual practice also (though there may exist in practice, to a certain degree, the inconsistency inherent in human society). It is not impossible to conceive peaceful relations between the two worlds, but these relations are contractual in nature, and hardly to be recognized as an integral part of the organic solidarity of the international community. If one of these two is imperialistic, aggressive and militaristic in its foreign policy, the gap between them cannot be bridged by simple community of legal forms.

The impossibility, because of antagonistic political ideals, of the coexistence of the two worlds in one international organization is very evident, if we consider the problem of the criterion by which the international court of justice is to give its decisions. Furthermore, as long as the principles of power politics and violence are maintained, disarmament or even the limitation of armed forces cannot be seriously considered, and faithfulness to promises—observance of the principle *pacta sunt servanda*—can never be expected.

In short, in every political unit homogeneity of political ideas and fundamental principles is required, and this is incorporated by every state in its constitution. It is exactly the same in what concerns the future world community, which we are considering. Each nation composing this community may or should maintain its ethnic, religious and cultural characteristics, but it should not differ from the other member-nations in its political ideas and principles. Nor can a difference between the ideas and principles of the whole community and those of each member-nation be allowed, because the former are but the common denominator of the latter. The structure of future international organization can only be built on the basis of a unity of national and international ideals in politics, and on the basis of the rule of a world law, which means giving concrete form to natural law, derived from human nature and therefore immutable and universal. The "Universal Law" advocated by Mr. Reves requires ethical justification.

We have to consider the realization of lasting peace as one phase of the gradual progress of human society. Faced with the present state of society, it is as Utopian to expect to be able immediately to abolish war as to think that domestic order can be maintained without a police force. The difference between the action of war and the action of police is purely conceptual, and need not much concern those who sincerely desire true peace. Even when a World Government exercises full power, we cannot guarantee that no civil war necessitating police action will occur. The problem is always the same: the evil rooted in human nature. We cannot adopt an attitude of non-resistance to evil, like Tolstoi and other absolute pacifists. To fight against this evil for the purpose of establishing true peace and realizing freedom requires a tremendous sacrifice.

Ideologically speaking, compromise and neutrality between the "two worlds" are unthinkable: *tertium non datur.* The rivalry and conflict between them will long remain. Fundamentally this antagonism is of the same nature as that existing in the spiritual life of an individual, and therefore the perfect solution of this problem, transcending mere politics, law and economics, becomes concerned with ethics, religion and history. It is ours to do our best to contribute to the creation of the peaceful and democratic World Community, in the firm faith that truth and justice will finally conquer the world.

The attitude which the Japanese nation, when confronted with the present international situation, will take, is not difficult to guess. The way for our people to proceed, the political ideals we have to pursue, are very clearly indicated in the new Constitution of 1946—which, on the basis of the principles of natural law, tries scrupulously to eliminate the former errors of militarism and ultra-nationalism from every phase of social life, and solemnly proclaims the principles of democracy and peacefulness. With great satisfaction we can affirm that since the conclusion of the last war the Japanese people have done their best to carry out the reforms required by this Constitution.

It is particularly encouraging to be able to recognize that the Constitution of Japan, in its fundamental principles, exactly conforms to those of the Charter of the United Nations and of UNESCO and the Universal Declaration of Human Rights. For the Japanese people their national ideals thus signify at the same time the ideals to which their international politics ought to be directed. For Japan the two kinds of politics exactly coincide with each other, and we have no possibility of choice about the direction to be taken in international politics so long as we "pledge our national honour" to remain loyal to the spirit of the new Constitution.

Japan, faithful to the democratic and pacific ideals of the new Constitution, should maintain the firm resolution of accomplishing her historical mission to contribute to the realization of true democracy and lasting peace in the whole world. Her special mission in East Asia, particularly for the time being, is that of collaborating with brother-nations to play the role of protective wall against the danger of Communist imperialism. By accomplishing her duties in such a way she can lay claim to the rights belonging to her by distributive justice, in the matter of raw materials, emigration, export trade, etc., which are vital to her national existence.

"Seek ye first the kingdom of God, and his righteousness; and all these things shall be added unto you."

IV

THE CHURCH OF ALL NATIONS

John Ching-Hsiung Wu was born at Ningpo on 28th March 1899. In 1920 he took his LL.D. at the Comparative Law School of China. Post-graduate studies followed, at the University of Michigan in 1921, as resident Fellow of the Carnegie Endowment for International Peace in Paris (1921-2) and Berlin (1922-3), and as Fellow of Harvard University, 1923-4. From 1924 to 1929, Dr. Wu was Professor at the Comparative Law School of China; from 1929 to 1951, Visiting Senior Professor of Chinese Philosophy at the University of Hawaii, and since 1951 he has been Professor of Law at Seton Hall University, New Jersey, U.S.A.

Parallel with his academic career, Dr. Wu exercised important legal, political and diplomatic functions: Judge, and later Chief Justice of the Provincial High Court of Shanghai International Settlement, 1927-9, he was a member of the National Legislature of China, 1933-46, Chairman of the Drafting Committee for the Constitution, of the Codification Committee and of the Foreign Affairs Committee; in 1945, Adviser to the Chinese Delegation at the UN Conference in San Francisco; from 1947 to 1949, Minister Plenipotentiary to the Holy See; in 1950, member for the Chinese Nationalist Government of the U.S. Panel Inquiry on the Conciliation of International Controversies. He was recently made a member of the Permanent Court of Arbitration at The Hague.

Editor of the Tien Hsia Monthly *from 1935 to 1941, John Wu is author of the following works:* The Art of the Law, Studies in the Philosophy of Law, The Science of Love, *a Chinese translation of the New Testament and the Psalms*, Beyond East and West, The Interior Carmel, The Fountain of Justice, Jurisprudence.

On 18th December 1937, John Wu was received into the Catholic Church in the chapel of Aurora University, Shanghai; and within a few years, his wife—Mary Teresa—and their thirteen children had all received baptism.

Christianity, the Only Synthesis Really Possible Between East and West

JOHN CHING-HSIUNG WU

I

Strictly speaking, John the Baptist was the only Precursor of Christ:

> The voice of one crying in the desert,
> "Make ready the way of the Lord,
> Make straight his paths.
> Every valley shall be filled,
> And every mountain and hill shall be brought low,
> And the crooked ways shall be straight,
> And rough ways smooth;
> And all mankind shall see the salvation of God."
>
> (Luke iii, 4-6.)

But in no part of the world was Our Lord without heralds who, to speak analogically, sowed the "seeds of the Logos" in the hearts of men before "the Word was made flesh". Unlike John the Baptist, those heralds were not aware of their mission, and yet God endowed them with wisdom and the moral courage to teach other doctrines, pointing nostalgically, as it were, to the eternal Word soon to be incarnated, the Redeemer and Teacher of mankind. Among such heralds were Socrates, Plato, Aristotle and Cicero in the West, and Gautama Buddha (b. *circa* 563 B.C.), Confucius (551-479 B.C.), Lao Tze (who was an elder contemporary of Confucius), Mo Ti (who flourished in the fifth century B.C.) and Mencius (371-289 B.C.) in the East.

It is no small wonder that these men of exceptional wisdom, whose influences on human minds are still alive to-day, should all have been born and flourished within the six centuries immediately preceding the birth of Christ. Their doctrines, it is true, are not unmixed with errors, and even where they were not erroneous, they were inadequate and led the human mind to an *impasse*. But this very *impasse* underlined the necessity of the Revelation; while the grains of truth that they contained and shared in common were but faint intimations of the Gospel, in whose light alone do they unfold their true meanings and real significance. In other words, what the pagan philosophers had uttered as desiderata are seen as reality in the Person of Christ.

We Christians must constantly remind ourselves that Christ is not only the Founder of Christianity, but also the divine Word, the true Light that "enlightens every man who comes into the world" (John i. 9). Thus the natural wisdom of man, the moral truths that every man discovers in his conscience, and the law written in his heart, come from the self-same Word who was "conceived by the Holy Ghost, born of the Virgin Mary", suffered in redemption of mankind, and founded the Holy Catholic Church. To know this as an abstract truth is one thing, but to realize it as a vibrant reality and to rejoice in the Spirit that it is so is quite a different thing. Since Christ is the Light of the whole world, the East as well as the West, whatever difference there may be between East and West can only be in the accidentals, not in the essentials; and we may be sure that such differences and varieties as we can find are permitted to exist that they may express the infinite glory of God to the fullest extent possible on earth.

In maintaining, therefore, the theme that Christianity is the only possible synthesis between East and West, our necessary starting-point must be the Person of Christ. Christ is the one Reconciler, reconciling men to God and at the same time reconciling men with one another under the Fatherhood of God. In the words of St. Paul, "For it has pleased God the Father that in him all his fullness should dwell, and that through him he should reconcile to himself all things, whether on the earth or in the heavens, making peace through the blood of his cross" (Col. i. 19-20). This is the fundamental reconciliation, out of which springs the brotherhood of all men. "For he himself is our peace. He it is who has made both one, and has broken down the intervening wall of the enclosure, the enmity, in his flesh." (Eph. ii. 14.) This reconciliation flows like a river from the fountainhead of redemption.

Our present theme can only be viewed against the background of the double reconciliation that Christ has achieved on the cross. Essentially all true Christians are *new men* in Christ; no more Jew or Gentile, no more East or West. What we have to synthesize are only certain qualities and modes of thinking and feeling acquired by the peoples of the East and the West in their different courses of history and perhaps also from their respective natural environments.

But before we deal with the theme, a formidable obstacle presents itself to our minds. What do you mean by the East and the West? Each of these terms covers such a wide sphere and includes such a variety of peoples and cultures that any generalizations about them are bound to be contradicted by realities. When you look at a people from outside, you are likely to think that all its members are about the same in character as in appearance. But the more intimately you come to know them, the more differences and variations you will discover among them. All types of personalities are to be met with in both East and West: introverts and extroverts, realists and idealists, the choleric, the melancholic, the sanguine, the phlegmatic, and so forth. All comparisons between the East and the West, therefore, cannot be more than impressionistic and must be taken with a grain of salt.

My own impression is that, on the whole, the Occidental mind works more methodically than the Oriental. The former goes step by step, while the latter jumps at conclusions. The former relies upon reasoning and experimentation, while the latter trusts in intuition and imagination. The former sees more readily the distinctions where the latter sees only the analogies. The former is more attracted by what is regular, the latter by what is exceptional. The former relies more on one's own effort, the latter more on Providence.

Bishop Fulton Sheen has made a generalization, perhaps as accurate as a generalization can be: "It is apt to be an error of the Eastern World to think that God does everything and man does nothing; it is apt to be the error of the Western world to believe that man does everything and God does nothing. The Oriental thus ends in fatalism and the Occidental in pride."

This observation furnishes much food for thought to both of the worlds. Only in Christ is the reconciliation between predestination and free will fully accomplished. The same is true, to a less extent, of the Christian saints. The East and the West will not meet except in the bosom of Christ.

Another interesting contrast between East and West is to be found in Father Gerald Vann's book, *Saint Thomas Aquinas*. I suspect that in his desire to call his Western readers' attention to the importance of the interior life, Father Vann has attributed a little too much spirituality to the East. However, the contrast is thought-provoking, and his conclusion that the East and the West are complementary to each other is truly encouraging and illuminating.

As Father Vann sees it, the East is to the West what Mary is to Martha:

> What, ultimately, is this radical difference of outlook which cuts us off from the East, from antiquity as a whole? We shall find its deepest roots revealed to us in the story of Mary of Bethany. People of the West are accustomed to despise the East for its inertia, its lack of enterprise, its inattention to what they regard as progress, the fact that the centuries have not made its streets any cleaner, its sanitation more efficient. They want it, in a word, to be busy about many things. But the East is ready with its retort. *Unum necessarium*: one thing is necessary; and the western world in its bustling concern for material things, its worship of material efficiency, its tendency to think of greatness in terms of captains of industry and grandeur in terms of material aggrandizement, has forgotten the better

part. It is shallow, and vulgar, and meretricious; it is busy about many things, but they are the least important things." (*St. Thomas Aquinas*, 1940, pp. 4-5.)

All this may be something of an exaggeration, but it is one that brings into sharp focus a real difference of outlook on life.

Father Vann further develops his theme by the analogy of the masculine and the feminine:

There is a useful analogy to be drawn between the divergent psychological tendencies of West and East on the one hand, and the male and female types of mind on the other. There are perhaps few people who are psychologically speaking wholly male or female; in the genius the characteristics of both types are united. But in theory at least the two are easily distinguishable. In the male mind there is predominance of reason, concern with the active, the practical, with doing; direction is centrifugal, looking to external achievement. In the female mind there is predominance of intuition, receptivity, concern for being rather than doing; direction is centripetal, the well-being of the object of love rather than the well-doing of other, external, things. And beneath this confrontation of reason and intuition, action and contemplation, there lies a deeper difference. The active, practical mind tends both to superficiality, that "externalization" of mind against which the mystics warn us, and also to self-sufficiency and egocentricity, to absorption in the question, What am I going to *do?* The intuitive, contemplative mind, on the other hand, tends rather to despise the just claims of the superficial in its absorption with deeper things; it tends also to forgetfulness of self, it tends to find its happiness precisely in self-loss, to make its chief question, What is *he* going to *be?* Consequently, in terms of religion, it is the active mind that tends to moralism, to reduce the relationship of creature to Creator simply to accurate drawing-up and observation of rules of conduct; while the contemplative mind puts before these things the quest for self-loss which is on an entirely different plane from ethical unselfishness, and in which indeed it sees the ultimate reason for ethical unselfishness. (pp. 5-6.)

But what delights me most is Father Vann's insight that these types not only may but *must* be fused if we are to be full Christians. To quote him once more:

It follows that, as each of these types of mind has its own specific richness and its own dangers, the soundest, fullest and deepest life is to be found in the fusion of both. There are individuals who achieve this fusion in their own personality; for others it is found in the fusion of two personalities in one, the cleaving of two in one flesh, which love effects. And as either in isolation is normally likely to lack balance and completeness, so East and West in isolation are incomplete, and need one another, complement one another. (p. 6.)

All this does not really present anything new from the standpoint of the Christian tradition. Who could have been more active than St. Paul? As the Apostle of the Gentiles, he was the pattern of all later missionaries. How full of toil and moil was his life! From what is recorded of his activities in the Acts, and from his own Epistles, one can easily see that from the time of his conversion, or at least after his return from his retreat in Arabia, there was not a moment of rest for him, right up to his martyrdom in Rome. In modern parlance, we can say that his missionary works were extremely practical and efficient and successful. But what was the secret of his sanctity and his lasting fruitfulness? To my mind, it was his intensely contemplative life, his close union with Christ, his mystical wisdom, and his spirit of love. In his second Epistle to the Corinthians, he revealed his internal landscape in a moment of self-forgetfulness in these words: "For if we were out of our mind, it was for God; if we are sane, it is for you." (2 Cor. v. 13.) In my Chinese version of the New Testament, I have rendered this pregnant utterance in words which are more intelligible to the Chinese reader: "If we are inebriated, it is for God; if we are sober, it is for you." But the important point is that if Paul had not loved God unto folly, if he had not attained to what Plato would have called "divine madness", he could not have been so perfectly sane and sober in his dealings with the world for the sake of the faithful. Only when our interior life has moved beyond reason can we conduct ourselves with perfect reasonableness in the world of human relations. Only when we love God without measure can we fulfil our duties toward men in the full measure.

All the difficulties incidental to the Christian apostolate arise from the fact that we have to live and work *in* the world, while all the time we are *not of the world* (John xvii. 14.) The realization that we are not of the world but belong to another Kingdom, should be the hidden spring of all our activities in the world, if they are to be of any supernatural significance, if they are not to degenerate into sheer activism, which is but materialism in action.

Of course, love is the bond of perfection; but love must be purified and sanctified in the truth before it can truly work wonders in one's own soul and in the souls of others. If love is not adequately illumined and guided by the true doctrine, it is liable to produce bitter fruits. If, for instance, with all the good intentions in the world, we should go to a country with the wrongheaded idea that all its culture belongs to the devil, then even if we should make a great number of converts, they would not be converts to Catholicism, but rather to Provincialism. This is one extreme to be avoided. We must pray the Holy Ghost to quicken our spiritual sight that we may never fail to see the light that shines in darkness. The other extreme is for a missionary to go to a country and as time goes on to become so enamoured of its culture that he is in reality no longer a priest of Christ but only a student of ethnology. Both these extremes, with infinite gradations between them, come from the fact of not being adequately prepared to be missionaries, not having delved deep enough into the inexhaustible heritage of Christian wisdom. This heritage is all-comprehensive; it contains all that is true and good and beautiful in the East and in the West. We need only to look at the galaxy of the Doctors of the Church to realize what a variety of types are represented therein. Among them are supreme masters of dogmatic, moral and mystical theology. But owing, partly at least, to the unbalanced development of modern technical civilization, mystical theology does not seem to have received half of the attention that it deserves. St. Thomas is important, but so are St. Bernard, St. Bonaventure, and St. John of the Cross. It is precisely because I am a Thomist that I regret deeply that the other Doctors' writings, especially those of St. John of the Cross, are so little known even among priests.

But frankly I cannot imagine how anyone can go to the East without being steeped in the mystical theology of our Church as well as in the dogmatic theology. How is one to cope with natural and pantheistic mysticism without being armed with true Christian mysticism? If we want to convert the East, we must first find the real East in ourselves, and I venture to think that the real East is securely in the bosom of the Christian heritage; but we do not realize it, because we seldom probe deep enough into the hidden riches of our Church, and all too often we live on the circumference of the spiritual life. Missiology may be of some help but it presupposes a great deal of self-improvement on our part.

In the great encyclical letter *Evangelii Praecones* (AAS, 1951, p. 521-2) our Holy Father has summed up all the necessary directives for apostolic works, whether of missionary priests or of missionary laymen. Just as St. Augustine and St. Thomas and others "baptized" Plato, Aristotle and the Stoics, so we must learn how to "baptize" the pagan philosophies of the ancient East and the modern West. As our Holy Father says, "The Church from the beginning has always followed this wise practice: let not the Gospel, on being introduced into a new land, destroy or extinguish whatever its people possess that is naturally good, just or beautiful. For the Church, when she calls a people to a higher culture and a better way of life under the inspiration of the Christian religion, does not act like one who recklessly cuts down and uproots a thriving forest. No, she grafts a good scion upon the wild stock that it may bear a crop of more delicious fruit." The Holy Father further says: "Human nature, though owing to Adam's fall it is tainted with original sin, has in itself something naturally Christian; and this, if illumined by divine light and nourished by God's grace, can eventually be changed into true and supernatural virtue. This is the reason why the Catholic Church has neither scorned nor rejected the pagan philosophies. Instead, after freeing them from error and all contamination, she has perfected and completed them by Christian revelation."

The whole encyclical letter must be studied and pondered and faithfully followed. For our present purposes these quotations will suffice to bring out the true meaning of "baptizing" the pagan philosophies and cultures.

2

On the whole the mind of the East is more intuitive than the mind of the West. Even Confucius, who is comparatively the most matter-of-fact and scholarly of Oriental sages, goes more by intuition and aesthetical sensibility than by logical reasoning. His doctrine of names, for instance, is really not a logical doctrine, but an axiological philosophy. He thinks in pictures, not in abstract terms. When he says that a father must be a father, he does not analyse fatherliness, but rather imagines a real father who would act in this and that way toward his son. This image is a mixture of the *a priori* and *a posteriori*, of the ideal and the actual. In all his recorded sayings, I cannot find a single definition. All of them contain a judgment of what is appropriate and fitting in a concrete situation of life. He does not try to formulate in definite words the principle underlying his moral judgments. It is only by reading and re-reading his collected conversations that you get to see directly into his mind.

A few examples will indicate how the mind of Confucius worked. A disciple of his, Tze Lu, once asked him whether he should immediately carry into practice whatever lesson he heard from the master. The master said: "But you have your parents and elders still living; how can you make it a rule of carrying out at once whatever you may hear from me?" But when another disciple, Jan Yu, asked him exactly the same question, he said: "Yes, by all means carry into practice immediately what you hear from me!" A third disciple, Kung Hsi Hua, took Confucius to task, by pointing out the incompatibility of these two answers. The master said: "Ch'iu [Jan Yu] is of a retiring nature, so I urged him on. As to Yu [Tze Lu], he is more impetuous than the ordinary man, so I checked him." (*Analects*, 11, 21.)

Thus, he kept his mind untrammelled by hard-and-fast rules, so that it could respond freely to the demand of each particular individual. Another instance may serve to elucidate further this point. In the time of Confucius, the official music masters were chosen from the blind. One day such a music master called. Confucius went to the door to receive him. When they came to the steps, Confucius said: "Here are the steps". When they came to the mat for the guest to sit down, he said: "Here is the mat." When all were seated, he said: "So-and-so is here; so-and-so is there." After the music master had gone, a disciple asked, "Was that the way of conducting an interview with a blind master?" "Yes, indeed," said Confucius. "It is the way to guide a blind master." (*Analects*, 15, 16.)

As a matter of fact, the way was the result of moral intuition responding directly to the exigencies of the situation.

Now, of all Oriental sages, Confucius comes nearest to the West; but even he seems miles away from its systematic and methodical ways. However, the average Westerner can easily see eye to eye with Confucius in most of his moral judgments. The same cannot be said of the other sages like the Taoists and Buddhists. Their wild and trackless musings are likely to mystify the practical intellect of the West.

For instance, I have heard a learned Western priest say that some of the Taoistic paradoxes in the *Tao Teh Ching* are "nonsense". The truth is that the typically Western mind moves in straight lines, while the typically Eastern mind moves in circles. I shall give some samples of the paradoxes of Lao Tze:

> Bend and you will be whole.
> Curl and you will be straight.
> Keep hollow and you will be filled.
> Grow old and you will be renewed. (Ch. 22.)

Truly, one may gain by losing;
And one may lose by gaining. (42.)

The greatest perfection seems imperfect,
And yet its use is inexhaustible.
The greatest fullness seems empty,
And yet its use is endless.

The greatest straightness looks like curve.
The greatest skill seems like clumsiness.
The greatest eloquence sounds like stammering.

(45.)

Taoism is not easy to understand. Its emphasis is on the indefinability of the Supreme Reality. It proceeds by the *via remotionis*, while Confucianism proceeds by the *via excellentiae*. Buddhism reinforced Taoism in its full exploitation of the *via remotionis*. The two ways, the one active and moral and the other passive and mystical, were never brought into a real synthesis in the soul of any Chinese, as far as I can judge. They were suffered, as it were, to coexist in the same soul as a result of compromise, but without any vital unity. Po Chu-i (A.D. 772-846), the most representative poet of China, though not the greatest, summarized his philosophy of life as follows:

Outwardly conforming to the moral bonds of the world,
Inwardly, I am free from the ties of life.

Like practically all Chinese intellectuals since the coming of Buddhism, Po Chu-i was officially a Confucianist, but at heart sceptical of the cosmic validity of human virtues.

Thus there is a schism, an unhealing wound, in the soul of every Chinese. Instead of achieving a true detachment, we have landed in a certain insincerity inevitable in such a dual view of life.

Only the Christian saints have really synthesized the *via excellentiae* and *via remotionis*. On the one hand they have lived in this world and loved their fellow men and performed their duties with the same intense sincerity as Confucius would always have desired. On the other hand, they have been as free from the ties of life as the Taoists and Buddhists could ever have hoped for. What is the secret of this marvellous achievement? *The Incarnation of the Word of God, and their union with him.* The Incarnation is the central event of the universe; human destiny hinges on this one event. This alone makes it possible for us to live in the world and yet have our being in God. This alone unites the transcendent and the immanent, and clothes every thought, action and word of ours with an eternal significance. The Incarnation is the only bridge between the *via excellentiae* and *via remotionis*.

In his earthly life, Christ has taught us by example and precept the way of perfection. This way contains eminently all the best qualities of the East and the West.

When an Oriental reads the Gospel, it is probable that his heart will first be touched by the ineffable tenderness of Christ toward all sinners, except the self-righteous ones. Our Lord combines an eminently feminine heart with an eminently masculine intellect. How many times he must have wept in pity of the infirmities and miseries of men! Even as recorded in the Gospel, he wept in sympathy with the sisters of Lazarus (John xi. 35-6); again, he wept when he drew near and saw the city of Jerusalem (Luke xix. 41-4). One of the most touching passages is what Our Lord addresses to Jerusalem:

> Jerusalem, Jerusalem! thou who killest the prophets, and stonest those who are sent to thee! How often would I have gathered thy children together, as a hen gathers her young under her wings, but thou wouldst not! Behold, your house is left to you desolate. For I say to you, you shall not see me henceforth until you shall say, Blessed is he who comes in the name of the Lord! (Matt. xxiii. 37-9.)

In this connection, neither St. Matthew nor St. Luke says explicitly that Our Lord wept, but who can help feeling that every word of the whole passage is a crystal of tears? To my mind, it is most significant that Our Lord should have compared himself to a "hen" rather than to a cock. His sacred heart is the heart of a mother—indeed, the heart of one more motherly than a mother. This is borne out by what God himself had declared through the Prophet Isaias: "Can a woman forget her infant, so as not to have pity on the son of her womb? And if she should forget, yet will I not forget thee." (Isa. xlix. 15.) Again: "Shall not I that make others bring forth children, myself bring forth? As one whom the mother caresseth, so will I comfort you, and you shall be comforted in Jerusalem." (Isa. lxvi. 9, 13.)

One of the most vital things, therefore, that Christianity has revealed to us, is the tenderest *maternal* love and care of God for the children of man. The soul of the Orient, if I may judge from my own feelings, is most easily captivated by this attribute of Divinity. Speaking for myself, it was the reading of the autobiography of St. Thérèse of Lisieux that opened my heart to the warm sunshine of divine grace. The saint of Lisieux knew the motherly heart of God so intimately and presented it so vividly that my own heart vibrated violently in response to the mighty waves of divine love. There was nothing sentimental about my conversion. On the contrary, it was because the saint focused my interior eye upon the *true* nature of God's love that my heart began to open like a flower to the balmy breath of heaven.

As to the eminently masculine intellect of Christ, I need not enlarge upon it. In my last book, *Fountain of Justice*, I have attempted to expound his philosophy of law from many angles. I have tried to show how infallible is his scale of values, how perfect his logic, how consummate his art of judging, how divinely appropriate his analogies and distinctions. He is the Sun of Justice, who is to judge the living and the dead. The King of kings, he is also the Judge of judges. What men of genius, what men of science, can ever fathom the infinite profundities and riches of the wisdom of Christ? All that the saints have thought and written, all that the Church has taught, has been drawn, with the help of the Holy Ghost, from the inexhaustible Fountain of Wisdom, the Word of God.

There is nothing that the human mind has discovered or

can discover which is not already in the Fountain of Wisdom in an eminent way. So far the East is more at home in the inexpressible, while the West is more at home in the expressible. But both the inexpressible and the expressible belong to the same Fountain, and the Holy Ghost alone can help us attain a living synthesis, because he alone knows the mind and the heart of the Father and the Son. It was not for nothing that the Psalmist should have been inspired to write:

> Clouds and darkness surround him
> Justice and right are the foundation of
> his throne.
>
> (Ps. xcvi. 2.)

This couplet must never be separated in our contemplation of God, for it presents a whole view. Without the clouds and darkness, justice and right would lose the necessary background. Without justice and right, the clouds and darkness would have no foundation.

But there is no denying that the spirit of the East likes to dwell in the clouds and darkness, being afraid that the cultivation of justice and right may be a futile attempt to confine the Infinite in the finite. On the other hand, the spirit of the West dares not even to lift up its eyes to the clouds and darkness, still less to plunge itself into them, lest its clear-cut notion of justice and right might be lost.

The only cure for both these groundless fears is to hold fast to the mystery of incarnation. If only the Easterner would see that true God has actually lived as true Man, that true God and true Man are one and the same Person, and that it is precisely because he is infinite that he could be made flesh, then he will understand that our only hope of perfection and divinization lies in faith in the divinity of Christ, coupled with a whole-hearted following of his human example. In other words, the Easterner should remember that true God is also true Man. On the other hand, the modern Westerner should be reminded that Christ is not only true Man, but also true God, and being true God, his words and actions during his human life must be envisaged in the light of his divinity.

In conclusion, let me say that in order to convert the East, we must know how to "baptize" the Eastern culture and philosophy of life. But since the most representative Eastern sages are all mystically inclined, we shall not be able to "baptize" them unless we first delve into a much-neglected part of our Christian heritage, the inexhaustible mine of Christian mysticism. To lead the East to Christ, we have to plunge ourselves into the cloud of unknowing; we must pray to the Holy Ghost to set our souls free from bondage to the material civilization and mechanical mentality of modern times. With absolute obedience to our Holy Mother, the Church, as our ultimate safeguard, let us aspire to the liberty of the children of God. The work of the apostolate presupposes on our part an earnest desire to be sanctified in the truth and to progress without ceasing in our own spiritual life. It is providential, therefore, that at the present junction of human history, both the East and the West combine in challenging us to lead a more interior life: the East, in that we must show it that the kingdom of God within us is the reality of which all its past philosophies have been but fore-shadowings; the West, in that only by developing our interior life in proportion to our material civilization can we transmute the deadening weight of matter into a vessel of the Spirit.

If the East does not find the West in Christ, it will not meet the West and love it. If the West does not find the East in Christ, it will not meet the East and love it. If the East is westernized, it becomes worse than the West. If the West is easternized, it becomes worse than the East. If the East and the West are married outside of Christ, the union will not last, being the result of a momentary infatuation; and they will only produce monsters. Only when they are united in the bosom of Christ will they love each other with the love of Christ, and their union give birth to "the new man".

Christopher Dawson was born in 1889. A scholar of Trinity College, Oxford, 1908-11, and M.A. (Oxon.), he was converted to Catholicism from the Church of England in 1913. Married in 1916, he has one son and two daughters.

Lecturer in the History of Culture at University College, Exeter, 1929-35, he was Editor of the Dublin Review, *1940-44 and Gifford Lecturer at the University of Edinburgh, 1947-9. He is a Member of the British Academy and Fellow of the Royal Historical Society.*

His published works include: The Age of the Gods, *1928;* Progress and Religion, *1929;* The Making of Europe, *1932;* The Spirit of the Oxford Movement, *1933;* Enquiries, *1933;* Religion and the Modern State, *1935;* Beyond Politics, *1938;* The Judgement of the Nations, *1943;* Religion and Culture, *1948;* Religion and the Rise of Western Culture, *1950;* Understanding Europe, *1952;* Medieval Essays, *1953;* The Revolt of Asia, *1957.*

Is the Church too Western to Satisfy the Aspirations of the Modern World?

CHRISTOPHER DAWSON

During the last four or five centuries, the expansion of Christianity in the non-European world has been associated with the expansion of Western colonial power. The missionaries went hand in hand with the European explorers and traders and conquerors who sailed unknown seas and discovered new continents or found new contacts with ancient peoples; indeed to a great extent the missionaries were themselves the pioneers in the work of discovery. Consequently it was inevitable that the peoples of the Far East and Africa and the island world of the Pacific should have seen Christianity as something essentially Western, as the religion of the foreigners, the Sahibs in India, the Hairy Barbarians in China and the White Man in Africa and Oceania. And so it is not surprising that the rise of the modern nationalist movement in Asia and Africa with its slogans of anticolonialism and anti-imperialism, and the reassertion of the traditions of oriental culture against the West, should be accompanied by a reaction against the influence of Western missionaries and often against Christianity itself. As a rule this reaction has not been a violent one, like that which produced the great persecution of the Christians in Japan in the seventeenth century. It has been political and cultural rather than religious. It has been directed mainly against proselytization and education by foreign missionaries, but it has also led to a demand for a strictly national organization of oriental Christianity and its emancipation from all forms of Western or external control, as we see in the recent report of the government commission on Christian missions in Madya

Pradesh, which has proposed that all the Christian Churches in the region should be fused in a single national or provincial body which would be completely autonomous.

Now it is obvious that proposals of this kind are irreconcilable with the fundamental principles of Catholicism. If nationalism—whether in the East or the West—denies the right of the Church to exist as a universal autonomous spiritual society, it is a challenge to the law of God and the kingship of Christ. But this does not mean that the Church is essentially Western. On the contrary, the same principle that forbids us to make the Church a national organization also prevents us from identifying it with a particular civilization. The mission of the Church is essentially universal and it is common to all nations and races—to those of the East equally with those of the West.

We must, however, distinguish between this ideal universality and the practical limitations imposed by history on the circumstances of the Church's apostolate. By the nature of the case, the missionary is in some sense a stranger to the nation and the culture that he evangelizes. He comes from outside bringing a new doctrine and initiating men into a new society. But however supernatural is his mission, he is a human being who has been born and educated in some particular society and brings his own cultural traditions with him, and hence, in some degree, his native habits and prejudices. In this sense it is true that the missionary tends to be too Western, so that it is his duty to divest himself of his natural prejudices and become assimilated to an alien environment and culture. As he must translate the Christian Gospel into a new language and speak with strange tongues, so too he must learn to think in terms of an alien culture and accept its social standards and values.

Yet this is not the real point at issue. For when men talk, as they do to-day, about the Church's being too Western, they are not thinking of this inevitable but accidental dependence of the missionary on his particular cultural background; they mean rather that the Church herself has become occidentalized: that her philosophy and theology, her liturgy and devotion have been so deeply influenced by 1,500 years of association with Western culture that she has become estranged from the oriental world and no longer speaks to it in terms that the peoples of Asia can understand.

Before we consider what grounds there are for such an association it is necessary to determine what we mean by the word "Western". On the one hand, there is our modern Western civilization, which has spread so rapidly through the world during the last century. This civilization is indubitably Western, since it owes its distinctive features to the revolutionary changes which originated in North-Western Europe and North America during the last two centuries. On the other hand, there is the ancient tradition of the Catholic Church, which may also be described as Western, in so far as it is the tradition of the Western Church and looks to Rome, the ancient metropolis of the West, as its centre and head. Nevertheless it is also a universal tradition, since it first arose at the point where East and West met and it derived its inheritance from them both. And if we look at the Catholic tradition in detail we shall see how this duality runs through all the different aspects of its life.

The Church itself, though it bears a Greek name, *Ecclesia*, derived from the Greek civic assembly, and is ordered by the Roman spirit of authority and law, is the successor and heir of an oriental people, set apart from all the peoples of the earth to be the bearer of a divine mission.

Similarly the mind of the Church, as expressed in the authoritarian tradition of the teaching of the Fathers, is neither Eastern nor Western, but universal. It is expressed in Western languages—in Greek and Latin—but it was in Africa and Asia rather than in Europe that it received its classical formulation. Greek theology was developed at Alexandria and Antioch and in Cappadocia, while Latin theology owes its terminology and its distinctive character to the African Fathers—Tertullian, Cyprian and above all St. Augustine.

While these men wrote in Latin, it was not the Latin of the Romans; it was a new form of Christian Latin which was developed, mainly in Tunisia, under strong oriental influence.

And the same is true of the new Christian Latin poetry and of the Latin liturgy itself. No doubt the Roman rite which has outlived and absorbed the other Latin rites bears an indelible mark of the Roman spirit in its simplicity, its severity and its concision. But this does not mean that it is only adapted to the worship of modern Western man, or that its spirit is alien from that of the East. On the contrary, it gives it a classical, universal and supertemporal character which is accentuated by its music, which is so remote from the modern West. For what has the Mass to do with Western culture? It is the eternal offering of an eternal priesthood—"without father, without mother, without genealogy, having neither beginning of days, nor end of life, but like the Son of God, continuing a priest for ever." (Heb. vii. 3.)

It is impossible for us to understand the Church if we regard her as subject to the limitations of human culture. For she is essentially a supernatural organism which transcends human cultures and transforms them to her own ends. As Newman insisted, the Church is not a creed or a philosophy, but an imperial power, a "counter Kingdom" which occupies ground and claims to rule over those whom this world's governments had once ruled over without rival. But if the Church is an objective social reality, she is not bound to conform herself to cultural divisions. She can take whatever forms and institutions she needs from any culture and organize them into a new unity which is the external expression of her spirit and the organ of her mission to the world. If this is the case, the question we have to ask is not whether the particular elements of this unity are derived from East or West—but whether they are fit instruments of the Church's supernatural purpose. If so, they entirely transcend the sphere of political nationalism and national culture.

Let us take the case of a typical Catholic institution—a

religious Order for example. Here the original institution of Christian monasticism was of purely oriental origin, and came into existence in the Egyptian desert in the fourth century. Almost immediately, however, the Church accepted this new way of life as an essential expression of the Christian spirit and spread it East and West from the Atlantic to the Black Sea and the Persian Gulf. And as it grew, it adapted itself to the life of the different peoples amongst whom it came, though it remained fully conscious of its origins and of the continuity of its tradition.

It was, however, in the West that this development of monasticism produced the most remarkable fruits. It was here, in the course of the Middle Ages, that there arose the idea of the religious Order as a specialized organ of the Church, dedicated to the performance of some particular spiritual task—preaching or study or the care of the poor and the sick, or the redemption of captives. Since these Orders are specialized, some of them are more adapted to one culture than to another, and it may well be that an Order that has been founded to fulfil some special task in medieval Italy or modern America, is "too Western" for India or China. But this is not necessarily the case. The essential principle of the Western religious Order has become part of the common tradition of the Church and is capable of being applied to the special circumstances of the East, no less than the West.

There is therefore no need to undo the work of the Christian past and to attempt to create a new type of oriental monasticism modelled on Hindu or Buddhist patterns, for East and West already coexist in the tradition of Christian monasticism, and the same tradition can bear new fruits wherever it is planted. The vital point is not the nationality or the cultural background of the founders, but the timeless ideals of prayer and contemplation and the universal spirit of the apostolate for which they are founded.

This, I think, is the secret of the whole matter. The Church, as a divine society, possesses an internal principle of life which is capable of assimilating the most diverse materials and imprinting her own image upon them. Inevitably in the course of history there are times when this spiritual energy is temporarily weakened or obscured, and then the Church tends to be judged as a human organization and identified with the faults and limitations of its members. But always the time comes when she renews her strength and once more puts forth her inherent divine energy in the conversion of new peoples and the transformation of old cultures. At no time can we expect this work to be unopposed, for the very fact that the Church represents something entirely different —the intervention of a supernatural principle and the coming of a divine Kingdom—must inevitably arouse the fierce opposition of all those human societies and powers which claim absolute power over man and refuse to admit a superior or rival. One of the strongest and most aggressive of these forces in the modern world is nationalism, and here Christians cannot expect to avoid a conflict. But the conflict is not really one between East and West: it is the old conflict between the spiritual and temporal powers, which was formerly confined largely to the Western world and has now emerged as a burning question in the East, largely owing to the introduction of the political ideologies of the West into Asia and Africa. But East or West, it is basically the same conflict, and alike in East and West the Church stands neither for East nor West, but for the universal spiritual society which is destined to embrace them both: "And the nations shall walk in the light of it: and the kings of the earth shall bring their glory and honour into it." (Apoc. xxi. 24.)

John Myung Chang was born on 28th August 1899, in Seoul (Korea). In 1925 he graduated from Manhattan College, New York. After assisting the Maryknoll Mission in Korea until 1931, he became Principal of Tong Sung Commercial School (under Catholic management), where he remained until 1946.

Elected Member of the Representative Democratic Council in 1946, and Member of the Interim Legislative Assembly (1946-7), John Chang was elected Member of the National Assembly in 1948. The same year he led the Korean Mission to the Third General Assembly of the United Nations and was Chief of a Special Mission to the Vatican. From 1949 to 1951, he was the first Korean Ambassador to the United States; in 1950, he was Chief of a Special Mission to Australia and New Zealand and Korean Representative to the UN Security Council (on Korean War problems). Prime Minister of the Republic of Korea from 1950-52, he was elected, in 1955, Member of the Supreme Committee of the Democratic Party, and, in 1956, nominated and elected Vice-President of the Republic.

His academic distinctions include Doctorates of Law honoris causa of Manhattan College and Fordham University. He is Knight Commander of the Order of St. Sylvester.

In addition to writing a Brief History of the Catholic Church in Korea, *John Chang has translated* The Faith of Our Fathers *by Cardinal Gibbons and the* Life of St. Gemma Galgani *by Fr. Coghlan, C.P.*

Three of Dr. Chang's five sons are studying for the priesthood, and one of his two daughters is a Sister of Notre Dame de Namur.

The Christian Contribution to the Social and Political Life of a Non-Christian Country in the Present World Situation

JOHN MYUNG CHANG

At first glance, it might seem rather unrealistic to think or to speak seriously about the possible contribution of a Christian minority towards the political life of a non-Christian country. The disproportion between the often very small minorities of Christians and their possible impact on their country is too great and obvious. In many cases, an even greater handicap besides the mere numerical weakness is visible: the lack of education and overall preparation of large sections of the Christian community for such a task, which is apparent in quite a number of countries, at least here in the Far East. Whatever may be the reasons for this situation, it certainly leaves us wondering whether and how our small Christian communities will be able to make a convincing contribution to the social-political life of these countries.

There is another thought that comes to my mind in this connection, a thought which may seem to point out just the opposite: the great prestige which the Catholic Church as a whole, as the great spiritual and religious organization stretching throughout the world, enjoys in the public mind of many of these non-Christian countries. This high regard for the Church may be based on her influence and prestige in the world, on her international position, her powerful resistance against Communism, her open and often challenging statements on international morality, noted by public opinion even in these non-Christian countries. And we may add to this the personalities of Pius XI and our Holy Father

Pope Pius XII, which have made a deep impression on friend and foe alike. We might also cite the impressive work of charity that the Church has organized all over the world, and the spirit of unity in faith and love amongst Catholics, which has led them to their heroic resistance and even martyrdom under the impact of persecution.

This great esteem for the Church in these countries is far out of proportion to the actual strength and influence of their Catholic minority. However, it opens a door for the apostolate of leading Catholics amongst their countrymen. It challenges all of them to live up to this reputation and the generally recognized high standard of their Church. But they will find this often a challenge and a task far beyond their strength, lacking as they are in numbers, in intellectual and spiritual preparation, and often also in the material means necessary for it.

THE RELIGIOUS SITUATION IN
NON-CHRISTIAN COUNTRIES

When we speak here of non-Christian countries, we have in mind those countries which never received any lasting influence from the Christian spirit and religion, countries in which until now pagan religions were prevalent. In them we find often an almost complete absence of true knowledge of God and his laws, a lack of understanding of the natural law and of Christian moral principles.

But these countries, especially here in the Far East, are not any more the "pagan countries" of the sixteenth, eighteenth or even the nineteenth century. They have undergone and are still undergoing deep changes in their social, moral and religious thinking and structure, under the influence of the secularist spirit of the nineteenth and twentieth centuries. The old religious, social and moral ties of tradition are being thrown off by the rising generation of these countries—ties and bonds which often were inspired by, and filled with, many precious values and truths of the natural law. The tragic situation is that there is nothing to fill this vacuum in the hearts and souls of the growing generations. The "philosophies" of secularism, materialism, positivism and often enough Communism, seem to offer the youth of these countries its only ideal in its quest for truth and moral values. This explains partly the great susceptibility of these countries to the false values of materialism and Communism. There is no hidden underlying Christian substance in the social-political life (nor, of course, in the private life) of these people on which to draw for strength and the antidote to the virus of infection by the dominant errors of our time. This is a fundamental difference from the life of the Western countries which might almost be called non-Christian in reality, but where nevertheless a strong and still powerful undercurrent of Christian spirit and thought is active and alive. In our non-Christian countries, the young generation is rapidly drifting into absolute religious and moral nihilism, and there does not seem to be anything to stave off or retard this dangerous trend.

RELIGION AND SOCIAL-POLITICAL LIFE

"Necessarily and continually, human life, both private and social, finds itself in contact with the law and spirit of Christ: consequently, by the force of circumstances, there arises reciprocal compenetration between *religious apostolate and political action*. Politics, in the highest sense of the word, means nothing else than collaboration for the good of the State (*polis*)." (Address of His Holiness Pope Pius XII to the First World Congress for the Lay Apostolate, 14th October 1951.) So many problems of the greatest moral and religious importance are involved in this good of the State and the people, that the Holy Father cannot see how they can "leave an apostle indifferent or apathetic". Of course, the Church as such will not interfere with the political activity of the people. But the individual Christian cannot and may not leave this most important field of social-political life "to persons unworthy or incapable of directing the affairs of State". The Holy Father warns against entanglement in the "contingent quarrels which envenom the struggles of parties", but at the same time stresses the personal and individual responsibility of every Christian to do his part in influencing and "Christianizing" the public life of his country according to the measure of his ability and special vocation.

THE ROLE OF THE INDIVIDUAL CATHOLIC

The individual Catholic must bear his share in this responsibility for the welfare of his people. By living his private, social and political life strictly in accordance with Christian principles, he will be able to exercise a stabilizing and elevating influence on the whole atmosphere of the public life of his country. He must first of all live, as best he can, an exemplary life as a Catholic. This is the necessary basis for any apostolate. But then he will be able to influence his non-Christian surroundings, Christianizing his own family, the groups and communities in which he is active. Through all these, he will extend his influence to the people at large, to the whole political, social life of his country. The Christian ideal, the Spirit of Christ, must come alive in his work, his words, in every opportunity of meeting and influencing people.

His task it is to "till the soil" in going among the people, to plant the seed and cultivate it, in the hope of a lasting harvest for Christ.

This is the personal task of each Catholic wherever he may be. This almost invisible Christian influence on the whole public life of a people is hidden, slow, yet penetrating and decisive. It gives supernatural strength to the more direct apostolic work of such Christian leaders as this people will bring forth. Without this foundation, their Christian influence on the people at large, on the political life of their country, will remain without its deep roots, its power to carry conviction.

The Non-Christian Country

The most serious issue that confronts the world to-day is that of tyranny versus freedom. Tyranny assumes many disguises, relying on false philosophies to justify its attack on human freedom. While the godless who would take over the world are always active, too many otherwise good people merely complain about the doings of their opponents, yet do nothing to counteract them.

Our daily life is deeply involved in, and affected by, the processes of government. But unfortunately many people are either not sufficiently interested in their government or hopelessly discouraged, because they are not allowed to assume their share in it on account of prevailing unfavourable circumstances. This indifference and apathy breeds official corruption. Negligence and failure to use the rights given by democracy naturally promote the rapid growth of dictatorship.

Withdrawal from the arena of politics on the part of good people will permit the tyrannical minority to monopolize the great powers of government, as we have seen in Germany under the Nazi régime and in the satellite countries to-day.

It is therefore of extreme importance that the right kind of men should occupy key positions of their Government, in which they can concentrate their efforts on the defence of God-given inalienable rights, guaranteeing freedom of religion, speech and the press, promoting a democratic development of the political, social and economic life of the nation.

The task of a Christian politician in a non-Christian country is indeed most challenging. Inevitably, he will be faced with many obstacles to be overcome, principally those of political and social evils.

Guided by the light of Christian principles, he must fight against these evils with great wisdom and undaunted determination. No one can exercise authority more directly and effectively in this noble cause than those who occupy government positions, be they administrative, legislative or judicial. Those in leading positions in the political parties can also positively exert their influence on the State, trying to weave Christian principles into party policies and urging the Government to enforce them.

Their mission can be greatly facilitated in various ways by the active collaboration of the people at large. The people must raise their voice to be heard by local officials, councillors and legislators; they must participate actively in local and national elections, join civic groups and be active in them for the preservation of the God-given rights of individuals and the nation.

THE APOSTOLATE OF CATHOLIC EDUCATIONISTS

There is no greater and nobler mission in the State than that of forming the rising generation. Teachers are the channels whereby the heritage of civilization is transmitted to the young, whose ideals and way of life will determine the course of the national and world future. They are in a position to set a pattern of good behaviour through their personal example and influence on thousands of students. This is particularly so when a Christian teacher is engaged in teaching non-Christian students in a pagan society.

The true aim of education is to train and form the mind and soul of the students, giving them a deep knowledge and understanding of truth. Good education must teach and emphasize the ultimate goal of life. The Catholic teacher in public or non-Christian private schools should strive to disseminate Christian truth in the minds of the young, impressing upon them that violation of the law of God carries grave consequences with it, that there exists a personal God to whom they will one day be accountable for every action of their lives. He should not only implant the truth in their minds, but also refute the false doctrines often common in academic circles, seizing upon every opportunity that presents itself.

The Non-Christian Country

It is a known fact that religious instruction is often forbidden in public schools, especially in non-Christian countries, because of the "separation of the State and religion". Apart from the few schools which are run by Catholics, children and students often have no opportunity to hear about the truths of religion. Even in Catholic schools religion is often not taught during regular classes.

Education's task of filling this gap should extend beyond the classroom, with the teacher as a guide and a friend to the students, collaborating with them in their school clubs, campus and student activities.

Youth is full of burning idealism. The revolt of youth, of young workers and students in the suppressed satellite countries has shown again their will for true freedom and independence, for something higher and more idealistic than mere material productivity and wellbeing. Christian educators and youth, steeped in Christian ideals, will be a power even in a non-Christian nation.

THE WORKING MASSES

The Catholic Church has sometimes been slandered as the "candle holder" for the capitalists and the aristocracy, having little concern for the poor and destitute. This sort of calumny is often repeated by Communist propagandists, but unfortunately some intellectuals also lend their ears to such accusations, especially in non-Christian countries.

These erroneous preconceptions can only be corrected through strenuous efforts to clarify the Catholic position as a true promoter of the interests of the working classes, pointing out that Christ himself willingly chose to be a worker, that the Church has rendered eminently great service to the welfare of the hard-working and less fortunate, throughout the ages and all over the world.

The idea of the brotherhood of men under the Fatherhood of God, which recognizes in every man his personal dignity and eternal destiny, will have a significant meaning for the non-Christian labour world. The social teachings of the Church must be brought to it, with special emphasis on the labour problems. Catholic labour leaders must propagate the basic principles embodied in the social encyclicals of the Popes and carry them out, as far as ability and circumstances permit.

In its early stages, the labour movement in some non-Christian countries is often under strong government control so that labour organizations are only nominal as far as their functions and effects are concerned. Christian labour leaders can contribute much here by rendering unselfish service for the benefit of the workers, as organizers, full-time administrators, labour lawyers, educators and journalists.

Most important of all is the basic motive and attitude of the Christian labour leader, who shows the wage-earner that the Church is vitally interested in promoting his welfare, that he has the right to claim fair wages and to organize unions to protect his interests, and that the sincere application of justice, good faith and fair dealing, is indispensable in securing an equitable realization of the natural rights of man.

TECHNICAL ASSISTANCE

The method of missionary work hitherto customary in practice in non-Christian countries often gave the false impression that the Church is only interested in the spiritual welfare of the people, overlooking their material interests except for some temporary relief services.

In the minds of non-Christians, especially when they exist in a condition of stagnant poverty, religion is often regarded as something remote and unrelated to their hard daily life. It seems essential, therefore, that the Church should prove that she is a true friend of the less fortunate, and that she is doing her utmost to promote their temporal welfare by offering actual guidance and assistance.

One of the most needed forms of assistance is that of technical training in various fields bearing directly on daily life, e.g.:

(*a*) Establishing centres where skilled workmen can be trained for various trades, as is done already by the Salesian Order after the pattern set by Don Bosco;

(*b*) Providing the necessary funds and equipment to facilitate the leadership activities of those trained by the vocational centres;

(*c*) Helping to organize occupational co-operatives, especially of farmers and labourers, and guiding them to manage efficiently to their own advantage.

Such projects may be started on a small scale, but should be developed in view of long range operations.

Closer association through these projects between Catholic leaders and the non-Christian peoples will definitely bring about better understanding and appreciation of the true spirit of the Church, and will render great service to the country concerned by raising the living standard.

THE ROLE OF CATHOLIC SOCIAL SERVICE

Christ himself performed many miracles to alleviate the sufferings of the infirm, which drew thousands of hearts to listen to his gospel. Thus the very concept of social service for all men owes its origin to Christ, and through this Christian social service the good tidings are preached to the poor for their eternal salvation.

The principal cause of social evil can be found in the godless philosophy of materialism; the eager pursuit of worldly goods; the desire for ever more possessions and pleasure; the ambition for ever greater power, which naturally produces countless crimes and evils, as we witness daily. If we cite only the evil flowing from abuses in the sexual sphere we can reckon up birth control, abortion, sterilization, divorce, concubinage and prostitution. The most deplorable fact is that some of these evils are even accepted as quite legitimate, are even positively encouraged by the law in a number of non-Christian countries.

The basic remedy for them can be no other than the

propagation of the true Christian virtues of sobriety, self-control, generosity and chastity. Catholic lawmakers, judges and physicians are conscience-bound to uphold firmly Christian moral principles in dealing with these problems in their official capacity as far as circumstances will allow it.

With regard to social service in the fields of medicine and relief, no other organizations in the world have ever accomplished more than those of the Catholic Church. This is true especially also in the non-Christian countries. Taking an example from my own country, I could point to the exemplary management of St. Paul's Orphanage in Seoul by the Sisters of St. Paul de Chartres over sixty years—it is the oldest of its kind in Korea. Another admirable service rendered here is that of the Maryknoll Sisters' Charity Clinic in Pusan, which treats, on an average, more than a thousand outpatients daily.

Still another magnificent service which attracts the attention of the entire nation is the Relief Service offered by the National Catholic Welfare Conference of the United States. Millions of pounds of food and clothing were distributed through Church channels to destitute refugees throughout the war years. The grateful recipients of these gifts did not fail to discover the spiritual motive of the donors.

THE POWER OF WORDS

The world has recently seen a most striking demonstration of the power of words by the Nazis and Communists, completely swaying people to their evil designs of world conquest. The advocates of the false philosophies of materialism, totalitarianism and Communism are making maximum use of press facilities for their propaganda purposes, whereas Christian counter-action is often completely inadequate to offset the evil consequences of this propaganda, especially in non-Christian areas.

To counteract these deplorable tendencies, a vigorous Christian campaign is imperative in every line of journalism.

Catholic managing editors, feature-writers and reporters can contribute much in presenting Catholic principles on vital questions of moral importance and unmasking philosophical fallacies. A daily Catholic newspaper, if such can possibly be managed, can exert a tremendous influence on the minds of readers, far stronger than any other kind of publication.

To cite one example: here in Seoul, we have seen the remarkable success of a daily paper which is sponsored by a Catholic corporation. This paper is highly regarded as expressing in a straightforward and courageous way the people's feeling and opinion on political and moral issues. The support of the public is so strong that the paper has the second highest circulation in the whole country. It makes a point of presenting to the public at large everything that is Catholic, and of propagating and defending it, thus skilfully trying to reach the hearts of the people.

Another quite successful undertaking, in the field of radio propaganda in this country, is the broadcasting activity of the Protestant churches. Daily programmes are skilfully arranged, intermingling Bible hours with light entertainment. Tens of thousands of listeners tune in to them.

Books, pamphlets and periodicals published for the non-Christians offer a wide field for our Christian contribution. Men of deep convictions and profound self-dedication are called for in this important apostolate of the written word. The papal encyclicals and other pronouncements of the Holy Father must be brought to the attention of the leaders of the country and translated into the daily language of the people. The Christian philosophy of life must be explained and made accessible to them. Without such a sound philosophy they will not be able to withstand the false philosophies of life: secularism, materialism, Communism.

This field of the written word is so large and the talents available often so few and little developed that, in this country especially, we feel acutely both the needs and the insufficiency of the means and men available.

There are many other ways in which Catholics can contribute towards the Christianization of the social-political
life of their people. But in all of them we need a deep faith in
the vitality and the strength of the "mustard seed". It will
always be the struggle of a minority against the overwhelming odds of superior numbers, means and interests.

The old socio-ethical and socio-religious order in the non-
Christian countries of the Far East is rapidly disintegrating.
Whatever natural-law values there were in them are in
danger of being lost in this process of disintegration. There
are no deeper philosophical, ethical and religious roots and
values underlying this crumbling structure. Man is being up-
rooted, individualized, thrown upon himself and his strength
alone to withstand the temptation of the spirit of the twentieth century.

These non-Christian countries are receiving at present the
full impact of neo-pagan secularism and materialism, either
in its veiled Western garb of "capitalism", or in its outspoken
form of Communism. By themselves, these countries will not
be able to resist the impact of this neo-paganism. A Christian
foundation has first to be built through the efforts of Christian
men and women in an almost desperate struggle against this
onslaught of evil. Only deep supernatural faith, selfless dedication to the task and a never-discouraged hope in God's
providence can support their efforts against the temptation
of hopelessness and discouragement. But this spirit of faith,
hope and charity will itself be the deepest and most lasting
contribution of the Christian faith towards the social-
political life and the future of these non-Christian peoples.

THE CHURCH AND THE YOUNG NATIONS

Our times experience a new strong resurgence of the spirit
of freedom and independence in many of these non-Christian
nations, a deep aspiration for complete equality for all the
newly emerging young peoples.

The world is growing smaller and contacts between men of

all races and nations are becoming more intimate. A desire for greater communion and community between men through greater international solidarity is evident.

This desire for closer union between men and the aspiration to true equality are only natural and legitimate. The Church's position is to do her utmost towards the fulfilment of these aspirations through her teaching and active support.

The teaching of the Church on the brotherhood of man under the Fatherhood of God recognizes in every man, regardless of colour, race and social position, the equal dignity and eternal destiny of the human person. We must bring this teaching of the Church more eagerly and repeatedly to the knowledge and understanding of our non-Christian brethren, especially of the intellectual classes.

No better example of unity and equality could be found than the Catholic Church herself in her teaching and practice within her own organization, and in her sincerely affectionate attitude towards the non-Christian peoples. The Church as the mystical body of Christ, the Pope, its head, governing the body, as the personal representative of Christ, and the members of the Church, as parts of the Body united in one Head, offer a striking pattern of unity and communion to the whole world.

This very real brotherhood of man under the Fatherhood of God is also strikingly visible in the heroic missionary efforts of the Church in pagan lands, in the selfless dedication of religious and laity alike to charity and relief works, especially when for their non-Christian friends.

The eminent position of the Holy Father as the spiritual leader of world peace, the constant teaching of the Church on justice, equality, human dignity and love, endorsed by her unceasing efforts for their cause, should become the most eloquent answer to the world's greatest need to-day—a spiritual rejuvenation.

Mutara III Charles Léon Pierre Rudahigwa was born in April 1911. In 1930, Prince Rudahigwa became a catechumen, against the wishes of his father, who opposed to the end the religion introduced into his country by the White Fathers. On 16th November, 1931, the young prince succeeded his father. He was enthroned under the dynastic name of Mutara, the thirtieth of a line of rulers dating back to the eleventh century. The catechumen's rank called for long and thorough testing, but the monarch was finally baptized on 17th October 1943. On 26th October 1946, he solemnly consecrated his Kingdom to Christ the King. In January 1947, he was made Commander of St. Gregory the Great by His Holiness Pope Pius XII, who on 31st October 1955, received the "Mwami" in audience, together with Rosalie Gicanda, his wife. (The king's wife becomes queen only on the death of her husband. The present queen mother, Nyiramavugo III Radegonde Kankazi, was baptized on the same day as her son.) The deferred twenty-fifth anniversary of Mutara III's accession to the throne was brilliantly celebrated in Ruanda from 29th June to 1st July, 1957.

(Ruanda, situated in Central East Africa, is part of the Trust Territory of Ruanda-Urundi placed under Belgian trusteeship. Out of a population of 2,310,000, more than 750,000 are Catholics and about 50,000 Protestants.)

What the African Soul Seeks from the Church

MUTARA III
CHARLES LÉON PIERRE RUDAHIGWA
King of Ruanda

It is an obvious fact that the African is deeply religious. To be convinced of it, we have only to look closely at his customs, which are, of course, undoubtedly mixed with superstition.

The African soul looks to the Church for all the moral values, the justice and the charity of her Christian civilization, for everything in her that is religious, and not specifically Western.

In a word, the African soul looks to the Church for the doctrine of Christ in all its integrity; the missionary, moreover, cannot present Christ's doctrine in any other way without betraying his mandate.

The African soul looks to the Church for a definite dogma which will give him certainty in his belief. This amounts to saying that the ancient faiths left the African soul in a kind of vacuum.

The mystery of God's love for mankind, created out of pure love; the mystery of divine Providence, watching over all men and over each one in particular—these are some of the mysteries which fill the vacuum of uncertainty in the African soul.

For the African, this creative Providence was, indeed, remote. In the Catholic religion, the African soul learns that divine Providence watches over every man so closely as to become at times almost a tangible experience. The mystery of the Incarnation, of the Redemption—in a word, the mystery of Love, for God is truly Love—fills to satiety the sensitive heart of the African, as of every "child of nature".

In other words, this religion of love, which offers a God, Creator of all things, and Providence of all creatures, a God made Man out of love for men, to redeem the sinful human race—this religion meets the need of the African soul, which knows only a divine Creator watching over his work from afar.

And what are we to say of the Incarnation, of the Redemption? It is a whole revelation which cannot but awaken the love for its Lord which is sleeping in the African soul. And once love is awakened it is only simple logic to demand the duty of adoration and service of the true God. Convinced of this overwhelming love which permeates his whole life, the African will henceforth be able to find God present in every aspect of his existence, where previously he could see only baleful influences, witchcraft and spells.

The African generally admits the immortality of the soul. In certain circumstances of his life, he honours the souls of his ancestors, to whom, in his ignorance, he attributes the cause of his misfortunes here below. Whence, certain sacrifices offered in appeasement. But the idea of happiness after this life comes to him exclusively from Catholic teaching, for the after-life is not necessarily associated for him with any idea of joy or unhappiness; he is in complete darkness on this point of capital importance.

But, if you speak to him of heaven, of eternal happiness resulting from his supernaturalized efforts to do good here below, his noblest longings and his deepest inclinations are, as it were, realized; for always and everywhere, the African, like every human being, unconsciously aspires to eternal happiness.

Among the elements which attract the African soul, and also assuredly the Ruandese soul, a privileged place must be reserved for the moral order defended by the Church. It would be unjust to follow certain psychologists or armchair moralists in making technical achievement the measure of a people's moral standards. Concrete experience and impartial observation have made short work of these theories, but perhaps not yet to a sufficient extent.

It would be equally onesided to canonize, as some have done, the "natural man". Men living in their natural state have their rough edges, which are not easily smoothed away; yet none the less they are not yet deformed by the refinements of purely technical civilization. In relation to the moral order, these deformities of civilization are not much better than the rough edges of the uncivilized; in fact, the contrary. The African soul, and especially the Ruandese soul, looks then to the Church for a purification of its own moral order, and for new values, as well as for preservation from the deforming influences of technical civilization.

The African, as is generally known, had a certain moral order, tainted indeed with errors and superstitions, but to which he was, and still is, attached. What might be called the two pillars of this moral order were justice and charity. It cannot be denied that this justice and charity did not always have the perfect focus of Catholicism; but they did have an object.

Justice between individuals, for instance, which was at times conceived as the severe repression of individual theft, should have been extended to all and have lost its savage cruelty. The African soul looks to the Church to establish such a balance by persuasive influence. Justice between families, once regarded as a triumph of might, must come, through the Church's influence, to depend on a better understanding of family rights. If the hunger for justice expects great things from the Church, as far as the African conscience is concerned, it is that charity may be refined and consolidated between individuals, families and peoples.

Africans, and especially the Ruandese, were inclined to think of charity between individuals in the form of mutual help. The sacrosanct duty of hospitality was thus its visible expression, and there were many taboos against various forms of selfishness. This superstitious terror was no doubt wholly pagan, but it must be admitted that the cause defended is a very good one in itself.

The Ruandese mentality looks to the Church to eliminate this dross so that individual charity may shine out in all its purity. And not only individual charity, but also charity between families, which must no longer rest on pagan matrimonial customs, but on a true Christian sense of solidarity.

What the Ruandese asks of the Church does not stop at charity between families, either; it reaches out to include charity between peoples. For political conflicts arise for the most part from a domineering egoism which excludes any thought for the good of a third party.

It is clear then that the African soul asks much of the Church in the moral order.

Its demands are not much less exacting as regards material wellbeing. Here allowances must be made. Many people look to the Church for organization, technical progress, and the practical realization of their material welfare. This error is especially widespread in our countries where, to make up for deficiencies, the Church's efforts for the good of individuals have had to overstep their normal frontiers.

Worldly goods and their immediate pursuit are not, however, the specific field of the Church's competence. We must look to her to lay down the moral laws governing the legitimate pursuit of these worldly goods. We must take example from her in this social order, but we must not impose upon her the irksome task of exchanging her supernatural order for the temporal order. She has neither the time for it nor the possibility of doing it. It is certain, however, that the Christian needs a certain wellbeing in order to practise his Christianity as a human being. With an empty belly a man has no ears for supernatural truths. The African looks then to the Church for clear teaching on this point; for a positive teaching, not a series of prohibitions; a teaching illustrated as far as possible by concrete examples. For the Catholic it will be intolerable to see that other religions are ahead in charitable action.

In economically underdeveloped countries like Africa, the Church's task in this field is more difficult than in civilized countries. The African demands much of her, at times without taking into account the lack of personnel. Children have always been over-exacting towards their parents; but in this way they oblige the latter to be equal to their task.

There is still something else, in my opinion, that the African soul asks of the Church: peace, the true peace which comes from order guaranteed by skilful government. This government is necessary if the Church is to achieve her aim and bring her followers also to their goal.

The African, and especially the Ruandese, has always proved submissive to hierarchical order; anarchy would be an imported product. But if this order is to be maintained on a reasonable basis, there must be a government that is at once strong and gentle, centralized and personal, national and international.

If there is not a strong government in every African Church, its members will think they are leaderless and their minds will be tossed about by uncertainty till they lose their right direction and their confidence. But this strength must be tempered by mildness if it is not to be attacked as a foreign power. The many-sided African mentality would recoil if there was any brutal manifestation of strength. Moreover, the main weapon of strong leadership is strict logic, and, if such logic follows the bent of the Western mind, this is not always appropriate as far as the African mentality is concerned. The African also has a logic, but he is more readily captured through his heart; a strong leadership with hidebound logic will not be as effective for him as a gentle leadership, permeated with kindly feeling. If there was a choice, it would be for the latter. Choice, however, here in itself implies a defect; what is needed is an alliance between the two things.

The second quality of this government must be that it should be centralized and personal. A leadership which changes according to the ideas of each successive rank of leaders is wholly ineffective. There is a Ruandese proverb: "Too many huntsmen make the hounds lose the trail" (*Abahigi benshi bayobya imbwa uburali*). The inner strength of leadership lies, moreover, in such a quality.

In the interpretation of order, personal initiative must, however, also be respected through consideration given to local differences. It is precisely the adaptation of a general order to particular circumstances which gives leadership the necessary quality of mildness.

A government which is centralized and not personal is just as ineffective as one that is personal and not centralized. The African soul seeks this twofold aspect in local ecclesiastical government for the satisfaction of its deepest aspirations.

Finally, the African soul asks that the Church's international character should also make room for the national idea; the Church must be everywhere adapted, without ever ceasing to be herself. We have to admit that it is asking a great deal: but what would otherwise be impossible must be possible for her because of her divine character. She must mould herself according to the characteristic differences of all nations without losing the basic unity of her doctrine. When the Pope proclaims this principle, he is only giving clear expression to what are the longings, however confused, of the African peoples. Nowhere can the Church afford to be exotic, if she is to keep alive. And so her local leadership, while its teachings remain of international scope—otherwise the Church would cease to be Catholic—must be integrated with the nation, if it is not to lose all effectiveness.

On coming to the end of this article, which sums up with inevitable incompleteness the aspirations of a continent, the reader will perhaps have realized that the situation is not the same everywhere in the various countries of Africa. I agree; and it is precisely in order to find more easily a common denominator that I have kept to general considerations. It will be easier now to apply these remarks even outside the frontiers of Ruanda.

The answers to Africa's longings are in harmony with the great aims of the Church herself. She is divine, and her Founder, who is the Creator of the universe, has wonderfully adjusted the response of his Church to the aspirations of his creatures.

It might even be said that the mass conversions in Central Africa are a proof of this predisposition of the African soul to the teachings of the Church. However, once the first ardour has died down, the difficult task of consolidation begins; in the refining process no detail may be neglected. At this point the longings of the African soul become rigorous and particularized demands, which, I am sure, the Church will know how to meet for the greater happiness of these young peoples. It is clear that they are working tenaciously for the fulfilment of their aspirations. It would be most regrettable if Africans were to place their greatest hope of this fulfilment simply in the various fields of modern technical progress; the Church must lead the way.

If the Church works untiringly to make this demand a reality, and does so before technical progress has dried up the African's unsatisfied longing for the things of the spirit, Africa's salvation will be assured.

V

TWO THOUSAND YEARS AFTERWARDS

Bruce Marshall was born in Edinburgh on 24th June 1899, and at the age of seven was sent to the preparatory school of Edinburgh Academy, where he claims to have been the first boy made to "stand in the corner" on Visitors' Day. Inability to control his mirth invoked this punishment, and this mirth, sometimes kindly, occasionally sardonic, is perhaps one of the mainsprings of his novels.

His first literary work was a collection of short stories—As a Thief in the Night—written in 1917, when he was a student at St. Andrew's University, and privately published at his father's expense. Of an edition of 500, 499 remained unsold, and Marshall still feels sorry for the solitary purchaser.

In 1918 he had to leave the University to become a soldier. But even the trenches could not still his pen. It was in the front line, while serving as a subaltern in the Royal Irish Fusiliers, that he began to write A Priest of Mars, which was completed in hospital after he had been wounded. A friend showed the typescript to the late A. E. W. Mason, who considerably offended Marshall, then "an old man of twenty", by telling him he required to grow up before he could expect to be any sort of a writer. However, Marshall now admits that Mason was right, and indeed goes so far as to wonder if, as a novelist, he has quite grown up yet.

The earliest work whose authorship Marshall is now willing to acknowledge is Father Malachy's Miracle, which was published in 1931 and written while Marshall was working as a chartered accountant in Paris and unconsciously gathering material for another novel, Yellow Tapers for Paris, published in 1943 and still explosively true. But Marshall's fourteen years in Paris helped him to see clearly, not only France, but his own Scotland as well; and when he returned to serve again in the army in 1940, the contrast prompted All Glorious Within, which, under the title of The World, The Flesh and Father Smith was an American Book-of-the-Month Club choice in 1945, as was also The Red Danube, published in 1946.

After a lecture tour in the U.S.A., Marshall went to live in the south of France, where he wrote the world-wide best seller, Every Man a Penny, the story of a French priest.

Other works include The White Rabbit, the story of Wing-

Commander Yeo-Thomas, G.C., The Fair Bride, *a novel of the Spanish Civil War,* Only Fade Way, *a novel about the two world wars, the novel* Girl in May *and an affectionate and humorous fragment of autobiography,* Thoughts of My Cats.

They That Have Ears
or
How the Church's Message is Received To-day

BRUCE MARSHALL

"Euntes, ergo, docete omnes gentes" were Our Lord's last words to the Apostles. "Go ye, therefore, and teach all nations." To-day, almost two thousand years after this briefing of the Church, more than two-thirds of the world's population remains un-Christian, and of the "converted" third, one-half are schismatics or heretics and probably only a tenth devout.

Catholics should remember this when they boast of their numbers. How many of our four hundred million lead better lives than Protestants? Are the inhabitants of Madrid and Naples more kindly than those of Nottingham and Ust Kamchatsk? Is it so easy to distinguish the children of light from the children of darkness?

Only a liar or a fool could pretend that it was. In France four out of five first Communions are last Communions, and nine deaths out of ten unsacramented.

As a Monegasque priest said to me the other day, "Il n'y a pas beaucoup d'inquiétude métaphysique à Monte Carlo".

Even in thunderingly Catholic Spain only fifty per cent of the population go to Mass on Sundays, and as little as fifteen per cent of the working class. Perhaps because they have Protestant opposition to fire them, Northern Catholics are outwardly more zealous than Southern; and in Ireland, Gideon's grace-soaked fleece, only about one in a hundred neglects his Easter duties. But of the whole bang shoot of us, baptized in Padua or in Oslo, girt with the armour in Lyons or in Rio de Janeiro, how many of us spend five minutes a year thinking about our duty to try to end hatred and injustice?

Fortunately all over the world a tiny minority of Catholics is beginning to realize that we cannot expect outsiders to be impressed by our claim to the truth unless its possession is seen to spur us to right wrong. Priests like the Père Daniélou in France and Don Giovanni Rossi in Italy are chiselling away at the tartar which centuries of nominalism have encrusted upon the Deposit of Faith, but there are still greater crowds to clap Coppi than to watch Archbishop Montini pontificate in the Ambrosian rite in the Duomo of Milan. It is in the United States of America that the clergy produce the most alert laity, both custom-made and off the assembly line: *Commonweal* is probably the most just and erudite Catholic paper that has ever been published; and the stupidest bumpkin in an American parish school has had hammered into him the obligation to forgive, for God's sake, the other bumpkin who treads on his toe in the subway.

A man not otherwise remarkable for his intelligence once said to me: "All our troubles to-day stem from the fact that Catholics love only God and Protestants only their neighbour." I never tire of repeating this judgment, because it seems to me to be profound. By confining their religion to the sanctuary and bottling it up in the street, Catholics prevent the wheels of the Church from going round. Let us make no mistake about it: it is not the liturgy in the common tongue which is going to make the invited come to the wedding feast; the Anglican Church chants the loveliest of English to the emptiest of pews, and the most Latinless lout cannot fail to understand what the monks are doing at Solesmes. Only when they see that our practice of charity is superior to theirs will unbelievers begin to take us seriously. Protestants might even forgive us our electric candles if we were to stop the bullfights. For Catholic cruelty to animals has probably hindered more conversions than Newman and the Oxford Movement ever made. If there is no metaphysical anxiety at Monte Carlo, there is plenty of pigeon shooting.

In spite of this hatred of Catholic callousness, Protestants are beginning to understand the Church better than they used to: in Britain our discipline compares favourably with the slackness of those who are willing to do anything for their religion except to go to church for it; and all the world over sectarian disunity is making the unprejudiced realize that Catholicism is the only logical interpretation of Christianity.

This is important: in the view of the agnostic philosopher, Protestantism cannot be true; Catholicism just conceivably can. Even Bertrand Russell, who is reported to boil with anger at the mere mention of an Anglican bishop, will controvert on the radio with the Jesuit Father Copleston. But we shall delude ourselves if we imagine that the un-believers are often impressed by our arguments.

Faith is superior to reason, but to say so and leave it at that sounds to the freethinker like cheating. To convince we must at least be able to reason our reasons for not reasoning. Very few unbelievers are in bad faith. Apart from a minority, glad to think that they can be unjust in this life without fear of punishment in another, most are anxious to be able honestly to accept the teachings of the Church. Such are not helped by unfair denunciations from French pulpits of the author of *La Vie de Jésus* as "l'abominable Renan". The attri-bution of insincerity to our opponents is the surest way of appearing insincere ourselves.

In other words we must meet the freethinker on his own ground. It is no good Catholics saying that Sartre's godless existentialism is false unless Catholics have sufficient meta-physical understanding to confute him. It is no use opposing St. Thomas of Aquin to David Hume unless we have read both. The assertions of the logical positivists cannot be dis-proved without a knowledge of the meaning of linguistic analysis. The attacks of the learned cannot be repelled by slipshod apologetics. Von Hügel's French confessor was right when he advised the Baron: "Ne lisez jamais les petits journaux religieux".

Of course I do not think that more than a very small

minority of the world's four hundred million Catholics will
do any of these things. I am pretty sure that the baptized
cads will go on goring animals for pleasure and the believers
expressing themselves less lucidly than the infidels. Indeed I
should be a heretic if I thought otherwise. "My kingdom is
not of this world," Our Lord said, and no amount of televiz-
ing ecclesiastical ceremonies will make it otherwise. Fortunately for us, God's arm is round the Church; as T. S. Eliot
has it:

> The hippopotamus's day
> Is passed in sleep; at night he hunts;
> God works in a mysterious way—
> The Church can sleep and feed at once.

Mr. T. S. Eliot's verse from his poem "The Hippopotamus" is here re-
produced by kind permission of the publishers, Messrs. Faber and Faber, Ltd.,
London.

Gustave Corçao was born in Brazil of a middle-class family on 17th December, 1896. His father died when he was ten. In spite of great financial difficulties, Gustave was able to complete his secondary schooling and entered, in 1913, the National College of Engineering, where he specialized in astronomy and geodesy. Later he worked for an electrical company and for Radiobras, an international radio company. In the meantime, he married in 1924, and this first marriage gave him two sons.

The death of his wife in 1936 awakened Corçao from his dreams as a Marxist-revolutionary idealist. After a long period of groping, and after his second marriage, he returned, in 1939, to the faith of his baptism. This spiritual itinerary is retraced in the book, My Neighbour as Myself, *first published in 1944 (Descoberta do Outro). Other books followed, translated into English, Spanish and Dutch; and since 1941, Corçao has been writing for the review of the Dom Vital Centre in Rio de Janeiro,* A Ordem, *as well as for various papers. In addition to his literary activity, he is Professor at the Military Technical College.*

What the World Expects from the Church

GUSTAVE CORÇAO

Before I go on to say what I really want to say from the point of view implied by the title of this brief address, it seems advisable to make it clear that so far as Catholics themselves are concerned, they see the Church through the eyes of faith and invariably expect from her what they should expect— i.e., precisely what she gives them. To us the word "Church" signifies one holy Catholic supernatural society that contains the full Christian heritage and shares it out amongst its members. She is the House of Salvation, offering us the Blood shed sacrificially for the first time on Calvary; the Ark saving us from the flood; the inflexible Virgin sternly guarding the integrity of Christian dogma; the careful Mother running to find her lost children and devoting herself indefatigably to the task of bringing comfort to those afflicted by the world. She is the Spouse without stain or spot living by the Spirit of the Bridegroom. In the light of our faith and the divine teaching of revealed truth we can distinguish two complementary sides to her as a transcendent supernatural reality. We know in what respects she must be absolutely rigid and inflexible and uncompromising, and we also know when she is able to adapt herself and be tolerant. As a virgin she can never relax her vigilance for a moment; but as a mother she must bear fruit, adapt and mould herself to circumstances, become a Greek to the Greeks and a Roman to the Romans.

Thus there is no problem, nothing to vindicate, as far as we are concerned. The Church is exactly what she ought to be. We expect from her precisely what she gives us.

In our faith, however, we make a distinction between the holy and infallible reality of the Church herself, and the sinful fallible reality of the people who are her members. We know that within the Church just men and sinners are to be found on every level. "I am a man," said St Augustine "on the threshing-floor of Christ: if a bad one, straw: if a good one, grain." Or in other words, as St. Paul wrote to Timothy: "In a great house there are not only vessels of gold and of silver, but also of wood and earth: and some indeed unto honour, but some unto dishonour." This distinction can help us to appreciate the difference between what we expect from each other and what we expect from bishops and Popes. Freedom of thought, even of protest, is immense in the Catholic Church, but we must never forget that the Church is a hierarchy and that we are therefore under an obligation to speak respectfully whenever we think we have anything to say. Nor must we forget that all our criticisms should be made in the spirit of that powerful thing called charity. But charity is a purifying, not a constraining or limiting thing; the citizen of the City of God is actually the freest of men. Without infringing in any way the spirit of this precept of charity the Christian may speak out plainly with a frankness unknown to any of the orders of worldly society, and may even launch out into frank and furious diatribes, as has happened so often in the case of the great saints.

But this is not the point I wish to stress in this present context of the Congress for the Lay Apostolate. Here we are concerned with what is expected from the Church by the world. Not that I can claim to have received any mandate from the world, to say what exactly its anxieties are. But I have had a fairly long if rather belated experience of it, and I should like to try to give some idea of what lies behind all the medley of suffering in the modern world, and also try to analyse the curious hopefulness with which the world regards the Church, even though it expresses it so often in such a contradictory and aggressive and even insolent way.

To begin with, I should like to point out that there is a harsh contradiction of ideas within the very concept of the word "church". In the eyes of the world—and in our eyes in so far as we are typical of the world—the Church is never any kind of supernatural society; still less is it a stainless, spotless Spouse. Seen from outside, in the light of ordinary human reason, even ordinary human reason thoroughly conversant with the tenets of the Catholic faith, the Church is made up of human beings, i.e., people who say that they aspire towards remarkable things but who in their daily lives, in politics, in business, behave just like everybody else, i.e., as though they were interested in nothing outside the ordinary things of life. This terrible discrepancy, which in our eyes is a reason for contrition, and humility and gratitude to God for his mercy, is in the eyes of the world quite scandalous. In this connection, however, there are two things to be noted. In the first place, we know that the horror felt by the world, thus scandalized at the sight of our general mediocrity, is less than the horror we feel ourselves, because the world is unaware of the real extent of God's ideal for us and only has purely human standards to judge our failures by. In the second place, we must realize that the world is right to be scandalized, and that the theological distinctions which provide us with valid reasons in the realm of theory are not sufficient to explain Catholic ineptitude in the face of social and political problems. The fact is that Catholics as a whole, both as a group and as a human type, do not make a very convincing spectacle·to the rest of mankind. In our own country, and in the fairly wide field of experience in which we lead our lives, there are some very admirable and virtuous people, and some excellent standards of value, and no doubt many people's lives could serve as models for others to copy; but the majority of Catholics, including the kinds already mentioned and many other kinds too, have no clearcut Catholic attitude to social problems at all. They may be quite decent in their private lives, but there is nothing particularly outstanding or effective about them as a group. And since the modern world judges institutions by the way they behave collectively, it inevitably comes to the conclusion that either the Church is not at this moment of history playing the part she should play or else she is not the thing she claims to be. The world sits in judgment on the Church, and the material for the gravest charge brought against the defendant, and the most serious evidence adduced in support of it, is all provided by the members of the Church themselves. Not that our lives stand out because of any noticeably scandalous or perverse behaviour; not that we are any fiercer or more selfish than anybody else; or any more immoral in our way of living, or any less fair in our dealings with our fellow-men. No, the greatest scandal of the century is to be found in the fact that we are just like everybody else! When the world makes its vague, confused, obscure charge against us, it is accusing us of this strange collective sin without a name. It might be said that the world is accusing us of—worldliness.

The modern world is going through a tragic period in which the whole of civilization is being transformed. The outstanding features of the general body of intellectual values that have governed the history of the Western world from the time of the Renaissance, and determined the structure of bourgeois liberal society, can be grouped together under two main headings. Theoretically, the whole of modern civilization has fallen a prey to nominalism and its derivatives, as a result of the state of profound discredit into which the intellect, and therefore man himself, has fallen. Practically, the individualism introduced by the Renaissance and the Reformation has led to egoism's being granted official recognition in the world and self-love's being exalted as a force making for development and social equilibrium, with a whole series of philosophies asserting the essential hostility between man and man, and man and his nature. Middle-class morality, the morality of "how it looks to others", the morality of prestige and success, has become the atmosphere, the historical dimension, enveloping modern civilization. The discovery of man that has been made since the Renaissance and the Reformation is the most tragic mixed blessing in the whole of human history, for it has meant that interest and attention have been focused on man's external and therefore less human characteristics. Thus, what is known as modern civilization has not produced any real aggrandizement of man, but an expansion or dilation, an inflation, of his external characteristics. He has puffed himself up instead of growing. He has stopped watching over, and fighting against, his selfish impulses, which the Middle Ages had regarded as the source and origin of all sin, and has begun to exploit the energy of disintegration, the energy of the ego. The modern world, with its terrible crop of neuroses, is the final and inevitable result of four centuries of nominalism and philosophies that have centred upon the disintegration of the soul. And throughout this tragic period, which has seen a mixture of truth and error, real achievement and profound disaster, genuine development and merely cancerous growth, throughout this whole critical period of development, or historic adolescence, the Church, in the sense understood by the world, has done nothing to defend herself against this process nor has she defended the world against it. She reacted against the errors of the Reformers. She defended her own doctrine, consolidated her own internal structure. But she was unwilling or unable to put up any real defence against the new values that were arising as signs of the nascent civilization. Errors were hunted out and attacked whenever they were explicit and clearly stated, but the unconscious life and the infiltration of these same errors escaped the eyes of the Catholic leaders of the time.

We Catholics know that the Church has no mission or revealed truth to guide secular knowledge with infallible certainty. We know quite well that the effects of this great historical misfortune have fallen upon our own heads and not on the Spouse who is without spot or stain. But this does not make the mistake any less serious, or the consequences of our failure or incapacity any the less deadly. The fact is that individualism, which was the very soul of the Renaissance and the Reformation, has entered into the Catholic world and left the mark of its standards on the souls of the faithful. Thus the Church appears in the eyes of the world as a group of human beings guided by middle-class morality and bound up with all that that implies. The Church, against which the gates of hell shall not prevail, continues to perform her ever-lasting and essential mission, but Christendom, that is to say Christianity in the temporal sphere, the whole nexus of historical events and effects caused by the refraction of the principles first enunciated in the Gospels, has ceased to exist. Or at least, has entered into a state of crisis in which it is being profoundly changed.

To-day after four centuries of individualism and middle-class morality the world finds itself at a scarifying turning-point in its history. In the splendid words of Mgr. Journet, "a new kind of Christianity is asking to be born". In the midst of its confused and semi-conscious anxieties the whole world is aspiring towards a new type of civilization. And at this critical moment what the world expects the Church—expects us—to do, is to shake off the bonds that bind us to the individualism and compromises of middle-class morality. Every day in the course of our apostolic work we come across examples of the way non-Catholics are horrified by the worldliness of our own society. I do not mean some particular —and fortunately rare—passing scandal of the kind exploited and exaggerated by the enemies of the Church. Nor do I mean any violation of the sixth commandment. I would even go so far as to say that it is not even a question of the way we support the flagrant injustices of capitalist society. What these people find really horrifying is the way the standards of prestige and success—the most anti-Christian standards that can be imagined!—seem to govern our behaviour as they govern the behaviour of the rest of the world. What horrifies non-Catholics is the way Catholics seem to lack any sense of humble pride in the face of the pomp and circumstance of the world, the way they seem to be so fascinated by all the usual signs and symbols of prestige and power and so ready to bow down before them. And that surprise is all the greater the more responsibility the followers of Christ seem to possess. The world cannot understand why monks who are running schools, for instance, imagine—rather ingenuously, as a matter of fact—that boys who come from important circles deserve special attention and that these important circles provide what are known as "the best people". The world cannot understand why nuns who live in such a simple way and take such drastic vows are absolutely delighted to keep special places in chapel for wasters just because they say they belong to some royal house. I am in the habit of saying, from what I have seen with my own eyes, that a charming woman is not the greatest spiritual danger any priest has to fear, but rather the presence of a member of the Senate or a minister of state. It is quite true, of course, that we are told to obey the laws, and people in authority, but there is still something rather strange about the delight Catholics take in doing more than they need to in this respect, especially when they show nothing like the same concern about helping people in distress. It is also quite true that the Church has to co-operate with the State if she is to fulfil her own functions, which are immense, but there is still something very strange about the extent of the servility to which this can lead, as has been seen so often in history from the time of Constantine onwards. The world is horrified—and it would be horrible if it was not horrified—to see what are supposed to be the freest of people running behind the coaches of kings. We are not, of course, anarchists. We do not assert the unlawfulness of all power. But nor are we, or at least we should not be, so gullible and submissive in the face of all the prestige of power. We know from our catechism that the Church and the human soul have three enemies—the world, the flesh and the devil. What is this "world"? Certainly not mankind, or any particular moment in history, or any of the institutions that are necessary for the common good; nor the world of men, the world of human souls and hearts. This particular "world" comprises all those standards that militate against human beings' transcendent destiny—the world of pomp and prestige, the world of pride in which self-love is an established thing. And the world of

men, the world of human souls, is astounded at the spectacle
we present in the face of this other "world", which has its
own "prince", the world for which our Lord did not pray.
"I do not pray for the world."

This world, the negation of everything divine, has always
been the great seducer. In the centuries before Our Lord's
coming, when people were still expecting him, the children
of the Promise always kept falling into this same sin of
naturalism or worldliness. Those who followed Moses
remembered with delight the fleshpots of Egypt, and the
Chosen People regretted the fact that they had lost the
security of slavery and all the pomps of Pharaoh for the sake
of dry desert and tasteless manna. Later, as we see in the
Book of Samuel, they decided they should have a king, and
their motive for repudiating the Kingship of God was
expressed in that dreadful declaration: "We want to be just
like other nations". The Chosen People wanted to be like
other people—wanted to evade its own transcendent vocation, wanted to be of the world! The Chosen People were
hounded by the great sin without a name, and went on being
hounded by it, until Our Lord fulfilled his own task on the
cross—from which we should deduce this ultimate standard
for ourselves: "But God forbid that I should glory save in the
cross of our Lord Jesus Christ." Even if the world may not
have read the Epistle to the Galatians or know anything
about the liturgy of the Invention of the Holy Cross it knows
in a vague sort of way that we are following in the bloody
footsteps of a God who underwent the Passion for the sake of
human beings; it knows that our flag is a sign of contradiction, it knows that we are supposed to be fools in the eyes of
the world; and knowing all that it is astounded not because
we occasionally commit some humiliating sin caused by our
own weakness and spiritual evil but because we go on living
by the same standards as the world lives by and glorying in
the same successes.

The moment of history we are living through is of colossal
importance for the fate of the whole of mankind. The

liquidation of bourgeois liberal society continues; but it is not yet clear, except perhaps in the Soviet East, what shape civilization is to take as it develops out of the ruins of the past. The only really clear thing in the world as it is to-day is the Marxist experiment, which, paradoxically, is the greatest and most thorough realization of the egoistic philosophies that came into existence at the time of the Renaissance and the Reformation. The Western world struggles on in its perplexity, trying now this now that, seeking new forms of economic life that will give some dignity to work, and new vitally democratic forms of political life that will help to dethrone the Machiavellianism of the earlier political order. And in the course of this dramatic endeavour the world expects the Church to give a clear demonstration of its rejection of middle-class morality. Catholics are called upon to labour in the temporal city, and in this immense task of building up a new civilization the world expects them to show an intense interest in the fate of the world and an example of detachment with regard to the things of the world. This paradoxical attitude, or rather combination of two complementary attitudes, is only to be found in people who have a knowledge of the values deriving from the Incarnation—the importance of life on earth (for it is on earth that we build heaven) and at the same time the fact that our destiny is not to be achieved on earth. That is why the Church can provide both a zeal for temporal work well done and a detachment as regards the standards of the world. If the first of these two elements were lacking we should have a Church which was not interested in human beings—which would be absurd; and if the second were lacking we should have a Church inseparably attached to the world, caught in the world's snare and so incapable of leading it in the way it should go. To put it more concretely, the world is waiting for Catholics to stop concentrating all their virtue on the sixth commandment and to begin to show some interest in the matter of justice in the way material goods are shared out in society, and in political behaviour. Above all it is waiting for this powerful race of men to give some practical sign that it has a complete contempt for worldly standards of success.

The impression one gains from daily contact with people living outside the Church, even those who seem hostile and aggressive towards her, is very curious and instructive. Through all the errors and confusion of the language they employ one feels that what all these sad and wounded souls expect from the Church, that is to say us, is precisely what we should be, or rather, exactly what the Soul of the Church expects us to be. It seems as though the universal Spirit who fills the whole universe is mysteriously inspiring the world, inciting it to ask us to be what we should be. Then the groanings of the world strike upon our ear as the indescribable groanings of the Spirit who dwells within us. We listen, and we learn, with those who expect enlightenment from us.

I said at the beginning that the world, deprived of the light of faith, sees the Church as a natural society and regards our faults as shortcomings in an institution that claims to be divine. And to a certain extent this is true. But now at the end we see that the world has a supernatural instinct, which becomes clear in the light of the mystery of Pentecost. And it is thanks to this instinct that the world expects the Church to be something different from any other society. It expects us to show by our behaviour that our vocation has an aim transcending this world. It expects us to be both zealous about the things of the world, and detached towards the world's standards of value.

However strange it may seem, the world expects the Church to be in the world but not of it.

Joseph Folliet was born in Lyons on 27th November 1903. He was formerly Editor of the weekly paper, Sept, *and its successor,* Temps Présent. *To-day he is Professor of Sociology at the Social Institute of the Catholic University of Lyons; Editor of the* Chronique sociale de France; *Co-Editor of the weekly* Vie catholique illustrée; *contributor to* La Croix, Témoignage chrétien *and* Criterio *(Argentine). He is Vice-President of the French Social Weeks* (Semaines Sociales de France), *and widely known as a brilliant orator.*

Doctor honoris causa *of the Universities of Montreal and Columbia, Joseph Folliet is a member of the Lyons Academy of Literature, Science and Art.*

He is founder and international song-writer in chief of the Compagnons de Saint François.

His published work includes essays, songs and poems, drama (Le Mystère de Saint François et de son compagnon, Le Mystère de Lyon et de Notre-Dame), *a biography of Marius Gonin, works on sociology and ethics* (Le Droit de colonisation, Présence de l'Eglise, L'Avènement de Prométhée, *etc.*), *and the recent volume,* A Toi, Caliban ... Le peuple et la culture.

"*The Gates of Hell Shall Not Prevail. . .*"

JOSEPH FOLLIET

That the world is to-day passing through one of the most profound and serious crises in its whole sublunary existence, a crisis aggravated by the phenomenon known to sociologists as the acceleration of history; that for the first time since man achieved historical consciousness this crisis is attacking the whole *orbis terrarum*, every nation and civilization; that on the intellectual side the existence of atheistic Communism and existentialism and the pagan totalitarianisms have raised doubts about an intellectual and social heritage which had seemed settled ever since the announcement of the Christian message and the establishment of Western thought; that in her pilgrimage through the world that passes away the Church finds itself caught in the eddies of this worldwide crisis, with even her very existence apparently threatened and the effects of the crisis raising such fearful questions for Christian believers, both individually and collectively, that they seem quite insoluble—all these things stand out so clearly that they have now become little more than platitudes. And if the Sovereign Pontiff Pius XII has chosen to speak on so many different occasions on so many different subjects, surely it has been, amongst other things, so as to help Christians, and with them all men of good will, to find an answer to the endless and unending questions raised by a crisis manifesting itself in secular organizations, established institutions, collective behaviour and the movement of ideas.

But does this mean that one has to concentrate one's entire attention on this contemporary crisis to the extent of letting oneself be hypnotized and almost paralysed by the frightening spectacle it offers? Does it mean that Christians have to withdraw into themselves and, despairing of all outward action, take refuge in prayer whilst they await the inevitable hour of judgment, a judgment which will be a condemnation? The speeches by the Holy Father already referred to should dissuade us from adopting such a pessimistic and ultimately sterile attitude. Far be it from me to seem to deny the gravity and acuteness of the crisis. To take, for example, merely the dangers of atomic power, this may be a matter of life and death for the whole human race, causing at the very least either unheard-of progress or unimaginable retrogression. Far be it from me, again, to question the novelty of the situation. It is novel not only in the fact that it is world-wide in scope but because of the extraordinary power that the discoveries in the fields of physics, chemistry, biology and psychology have now conferred upon men; the sudden irruption of a technical, industrial, urban civilization based on the written and spoken word and the photographic image and extending over the surface of the whole earth; the rapid unification and in fact "uniformation" of mankind; the transformation of acts formerly determined biologically or socially into works of the reflective intelligence and free will; the conscious responsibility for history that has now devolved upon every single human being; and finally the inescapable alternatives that will bear no half-measures—God or nothing—imposed upon every thinking person by the spread of atheism in various practical and theoretical forms.

But when the historian casts an eye back upon the past he finds situations there which, while not identical with our own, for history never repeats itself, nevertheless provide striking analogies with it. Comparisons are not the same thing as reasons, but comparisons may provide reasons for hope. Historical perspective gives the facts and anxieties of our own day their true proportions. In the case of small minds, which are usually what La Bruyère used to call violent minds, it can lead to scepticism; in others, of the kind that are always longing for easy comfort, the stupid optimism of "It'll be all right in the end." But to strong and upright spirits the historical perspective can give that manly confidence which is not to be confused with hope in the theological sense but is a sort of offshoot of it. It does not matter much whether you talk about active pessimism as Koestler does, or, as I should prefer to call it, clear-headed optimism; what matters in the end is the clearness of the head and the activity.

We are moving in a period of crisis, true. But looking through the Christian literature of the past, studying the sermons that have been preached, the annals and diaries that have been kept, the spiritual writings that have been written, one gains the impression, rightly or wrongly, that there has always been a crisis, that Christians have always lived in a world in a state of continual crisis. It is always the same thing—tears over the misery of the time, the triumph of sin and error, the absence of faith and charity, even speculations as to the end of the world, felt as imminent and catastrophic, so overflowing is the cup of God's anger. Even comparatively happy periods, which from a distance give the impression of having been calm and stable, even the "ages of faith", have produced groans and imprecations. Let us make all due allowance for exaggeration, bad temper, literary cliché; nevertheless it would be a mistake to look upon the anxieties experienced by our forebears with a pitying and almost disdainful eye. There were serious reasons for them and they were all too real. Even in peaceful times they were often based on the perception of real dangers which later revealed themselves in all their violence. In the thick of the seventeenth century, for instance, surely Bossuet is the voice of the storm destined to break in the eighteenth?

But there have been moments in history when these anxieties were only too well founded, when they arose from inescapable daily observations, when the future seemed definitely closed, with no—from the purely human point of view—possible way out. They had such a powerful drive behind them that in the attempt to escape from them many very gifted minds were forced to envisage the end of the world; consciences, sometimes very pure consciences, despaired of any general salvation, and became too closely concerned with their own personal salvation, and took refuge in an inner life which was not always without its illusions; while less sturdy or self-controlled spirits sought "compensations", as the psychologists say, in the artificial warmth of "spiritual" or "end-of-the-world" sects—not to mention such phenomena as the morbid orgies of the witches' sabbaths in the fifteenth century or the deceptive certainties of the occult believers of the sixteenth.

It would be paradoxical to say that the Church has never known any world except one in a state of crisis. But conversely it would mean ignoring history to idealize the past to the point of turning it into a Virgilian idyll. The Church has faced many crises since she first came into existence; she has on more than one occasion seemed to be swallowed up by the waves; and each time she has escaped shipwreck and re-embarked on her way to the future, to the stupefaction of those who judge her by purely human standards, and even of Christians when they have been unenlightened by hope.

Was she not born into a world of crisis? Nothing could have been more ordered, or so it seemed, more rich and prosperous, more solid, than that Roman Empire whose remains still fill us with astonishment when we come upon them in what were once small colonial towns—Baalbek, El-Djem, Timgad, Volubilis. But behind all the pomp and circumstance there was a crisis brewing—a political crisis, which was to end, despite all Augustus's efforts at reform, in the replacement of the old Romans by new men barely freed from slavery, and of the Roman legions by barbarian mercenaries; an economic and social crisis which was to lead to the pernickety totalitarianism and petty-minded supervision of the Dalmatian Emperors; and above all a spiritual crisis, in which Christianity was involved up to the hilt. With the unification of the Mediterranean world and the advances made by the spirit of scepticism, the old Graeco-Roman paganism burst out everywhere. A universal religion was being sought for, one which was at the same time a personal religion, and there was no lack of candidates to take the place of the old paganism—philosophies tinged with religion, Stoicism, neo-Platonism, neo-Pythagoreanism; occult faiths like the dangerous Gnosis; mystery religions; universalist religions, proselytizing Judaism, Mithraism, Manicheism; the civic religion of Rome and Augustus imposed by the soldiers and executioners and given new life by the theurgic neo-Platonism of Julian the Apostate. Nothing seemed specially favourable to the victory of Christianity: Greek sensibility, Roman realism, Jewish hostility, the haughty scepticism of the intellectuals, these forces and many more all seemed ranged against it. And yet it emerged victorious. It came out of the crisis as the one real victor.

But no sooner was the brief respite afforded by the Edict of Milan over than Christianity entered upon another crisis. To-day we are inclined to underestimate the importance of the Arian crisis and to regard it as having been no more than a difference of theological opinion. We tend to ignore its many repercussions—racial, cultural, social and political. We do not sufficiently realize that it was in many ways a subtle return to paganism, and as such warmly welcomed by Greek rationalism and the insufficiently baptized paganism of the barbarian Goths and Vandals; and at the same time an equally subtle foretaste of the monotheism of Islam. As has been said, in words that have become famous, the world woke up and found, with a shiver, that it was Arian. And it nearly remained Arian; which would have made it pagan— a purified kind of paganism, no doubt, tinctured with Christianity, but a prey to every kind of intellectual temptation because deprived of the God Christ. And yet, thanks to the tenacity of a few Christians, bishops, priests, laymen, the Church surmounted this trial for ever. It was a victory that had been won by a hair's breadth.

The crisis that followed, in the West, lasted for centuries—the "centuries of faith", as Emile Gebhart would call them, which saw the total subversion of the Roman Empire, the barbarian invasions and consequent settlements, a frightful retrogression from the point of view of civilization and general morality, and the slow, haphazard development of feudalism. Apart from a few brief intervals of comparative splendour like the Carolingian Renaissance, the Church might seem to have been submerged by barbarism, or rather made one with it. Great historians like Godefroy Kurth and Christopher Dawson have shown how she freed herself from it and how, not satisfied with merely recovering her own spiritual freedom, she shaped and moulded the whole world of barbarism, either by direct action or by taking over temporal activities, and finally produced what we now know as Western civilization. When the Roman Empire crumbled into ruin there were a number of people who denounced the crimes committed by the great She-Wolf and considered that with the end of Rome would come the end of the world. And it is not difficult to appreciate their attitude when one remembers that they lived in a period of almost total darkness lit only by the feeble glimmer of an intellectual light dating from days long past. And yet it was only the end of one kind of world, on the ruins of which there was to arise, new creation following new creation, Renaissance following Renaissance, a wholly new one.

In the building up of this new civilization a decisive part was played by the monks—the sons of St. Martin and St. Columba, Benedictines, Cluniacs, Cistercians, all engaged in restoring and renewing. By a drastic paradox it was the very people who had fled the world who did most to save it in the temporal sphere. They restored the countrysides of the West that had been ruined by war and neglect. They found a shelter for the treasures of graphic art. They gave feudalism, which in its early stages, as Marc Bloch has shown, was like a gigantic mutual aid society, the purest part of its spirit and the most authentic models on which its ultimate achievements were based. Once again spirit had mastered chaos.

It was in these dark ages that there took place one of the most astonishing and most important revolutions in history—the disappearance of personal slavery. There has been a great deal of debate and discussion about the causes of this great event, which seems now to have taken place once and for all. We know now that these causes derived from two utterly different orders—one material and technical, the enormous amount of energy released by the development of the use of horses and watermills, the other moral and spiritual, the Christian respect for the pre-eminent dignity of the human person. These two interacting motive forces combined to lead mankind forward along the way of progress.

In the new Europe, the return of an urban civilization, the growth of a commercial and industrial middle class, its rivalry with the great feudal barons, both lay and ecclesiastical, the revival of Latin and Roman law, the rediscovery of Greek philosophy and in particular of Aristotle, the spiritual pretensions of the Holy Empire, the rise of the new nationalist feelings—all these things were to lead to a new crisis whose full scope and depth and persistence are sometimes veiled from us by a too departmentalized conception of human history. The quarrel over investitures, the conflict between the Empire and the Papacy, the advance of the city communes and their skirmishes with the lords, ecclesiastical and lay, the Peasants' Wars and risings, Latin Averroism, Albigensian Catharism, the various heresies affecting to some extent or other the people living in towns, especially the weavers, are all manifestations of the same crisis, all touching and interacting upon each other—economic, religious, intellectual, ideological, spiritual. This interaction helps to explain, of course, the many confusions and inconsistencies. In this drama, with its hundred and one acts, the feudal organizations that had given the Church a moment's peace were to turn out a dangerous, almost mortal, embarrassment. Beginning as a shield and buckler, they developed into an encrustation from which the Church had to be freed by the Holy Spirit. When we add, from the outside, the inroads made by the Mongols and the assaults of the Mohammedan Turk, an infinitely more dangerous enemy than Arab Islam, we begin to get some faint idea of the dangers threatening the Church.

Because of its well-nigh complete disappearance and the air of mystery in which it has always been wrapped, Catharism has now become little more than a curiosity. Many historians tend to regard it as merely another form of heresy. We find it difficult to imagine what a menace this counter-Church, which included both Manicheism and Gnosticism amongst its origins, was to the true Church, to Western culture and in fact to the whole of civilization—for no country in the world seems to have been able to endure or absorb that essentially anti-social thing, Manichean dualism. The nobility and the middle classes both in their turn looked to it to provide them with ideological weapons in the struggle they waged against the ecclesiastical forces they identified with feudal power. And the same is true of all the other heresies on the Patarine or a Vaudois model.

And yet from this dangerous situation the Church emerged triumphant. She succeeded in asserting her spiritual liberty in the face of Emperors, kings and feudal lords. She succeeded in giving a Christian tone to the advance of the communes and in educating the rising middle classes in the way they should go by means of guilds and corporations. From the very circles most infected with Catharism and heresy she produced the powerful religious current of the Mendicant and Third Orders. When Christian thought seemed to have reached an impasse with the controversy between Abelard and St. Bernard, a synthesis began to be achieved between the thought of the Ancients and Christian thought in the great days of the scholastics, with its shining firmament of stars, Albert the Great and Alexander of Hales,

St. Thomas Aquinas and St. Bonaventure. The great figures of St. Francis and St. Dominic dominate this vital, hectic age as the cathedrals dominated the cities.

Another step had been achieved. Another state of balance had been found.

It was to be of short duration, for a period of disequilibrium was beginning in which Europe, and with Europe the Church, were to undergo fearful trials. In practice it was one single crisis, with a few brief intervals, dating from the time of the Hundred Years' War and the Great Schism to the end of the Wars of Religion. This did not reach everywhere in Europe at the same time, nor did it affect all parts to the same extent, but it went on incessantly until a new state of equilibrium was reached.

The Hundred Years' War, the Wars of the Roses, the Great Schism in the West, the great peasant risings in France, England and Germany, the Black Death, the heresies associated with the Lollards and the names of Wycliff and Huss, the waves of false mysticism, the social convulsions setting nobility against middle class and the upper levels of the people against the lower, the witches' sabbaths, the revival of black magic and the burnings at the stake used to put it down, the successive waves of Protestantism, the first symptoms of freethinking and freeliving, the nationalist wars, frightful outbursts of immorality and cruelty—all these things characterize a period affected at one and the same time by the joint rise of capitalism and the middle classes, the growth of the nations we know to-day and the nationalism which was its inevitable result, the longing for, and the effects of, the great new geographical discoveries, the individualism of the Renaissance and the Reformation, the systematization of the inner life and psychological introspection—in short a prodigious transformation of intellectual culture.

From this conflict the Church was to emerge crippled but once again victorious. The Spanish Golden Age, French classicism, the Council of Trent and the Counter-Reformation are all signs of this victory.

But it was to be a short respite, for the end of the eighteenth century saw both the invasion of "philosophical" unbelief known as the Enlightenment, and finally the violent explosion of the French Revolution, which was followed by a whole series of revolutions, liberal, anti-clerical, in fact anti-Christian, throughout the whole world. With the successive captivities of Pius VI and Pius VII and the crowning of the Goddess of Reason in Notre Dame in Paris the Church seemed as good as dead, and in point of fact the people whose motto was *écrasons l'infâme* were not backward in embalming her. This apparent collapse of the Church coincided with one of the acutest periods of growing pains that mankind has ever experienced. It included a dual revolution, both technical and economic, in industry and agriculture; the change-over from financial to industrial capitalism; the final overthrow of the nobility and, temporally speaking, the priesthood, by the middle classes; the ascendancy of mathematics, physics and chemistry in the field of knowledge, with "scientism", materialism and positivism providing them with a sort of provisional escort; the arrival of parliamentary democracy and universal suffrage throughout the civilized world; the definite establishment of a civilization based on the spoken word, symbolized by the success of the press; the grouping of nations into new national units in Europe and America; the humanitarian ideology of the Freemasons; the tentative haphazard beginnings of socialism and the working-class movement.

Christians to-day have forgotten what a state of religious chaos Europe was left in after the French Revolution and the torment of the Napoleonic era. A dearth of priests (and those there were badly educated and often late vocations), a lack of religious Orders, an almost total absence of any higher Catholic education, a theology all too often contaminated by Romanticism, a "liberal" middle class with Voltaire as its god, regarding religion as a thing for peasants and women and children—who did in fact form the majority of Catholic believers—a new world of working people all growing up outside the Church, a soulless economy developing apart from any Christian influence, governments pestering, in fact persecuting, Christianity, or else simply using it for their own unpleasant ends—such are the main features of the picture.

This was the situation that within a century the Church was to retrieve in Europe at the same time as she was achieving unprecedented success in the missionary field in all four quarters of the globe. The recovery was not to be without its difficulties, of course—not without external conflicts or internal pangs: one only needs to remember the *Kult.. kampf* and Hitler's persecutions in Germany, Combism in France, the painful episodes centring round Modernism and the *Action Française*, and all the innumerable difficulties hampering the development of the Catholic social movement, to appreciate the stiffness of the ascent facing the Church. But in the end she achieved the state of shining splendour and almost universal respect—excepting the Communist world— which mark the pontificates of Popes Pius XI and Pius XII.

The above snapshots of these various crises, given sharper emphasis by their having been perforce lumped together in far too narrow a compass, this picture of the Church's successive interments and no less successive resurrections, seems likely, it seems to me, to give rise to two different kinds of temptation, which in actual fact result in the same thing— passivity. On the one hand there may be a sceptical, static pessimism, manifesting itself as "Oh, what's the use?"— what's the use of getting upset about things or trying to do anything about them when the whole history of Christianity has always meant simply going on through a continual series of trials and miseries which have only varied superficially, in appearance? On the other hand there is a kind of optimism which can be very nice for one's intellectual comfort, based on the attitude that ultimately the Church is always bound to come out of the most atrocious kinds of tribulations purer and more vital than she ever was before, and the only thing you need, to make the present and the future and the whole of eternity absolutely safe, is the protection of God. In both cases the end is a *quieta non movere* favourable to every kind of failure and refusal to do anything.

It means forgetting that though every age may be critical in some way or other there is nevertheless a difference between times of acute crisis and times of stability, calm periods and troubled periods, ages of construction and ages of disintegration, moments of apparent defeat and moments of evident triumph. There are falls, rises, lulls. There are catacomb eras, basilica eras, cathedral eras. In the religious field as in all others, acting on the assumption that all is for the worst in the worst of all possible worlds is the worst kind of action. We must keep to the way of the Cross, but we must go on hoping and seeking for the Resurrection and the life of glory.

It also means forgetting that the Church, surrounded and weighed down as she is by crisis after crisis, can never be saved except by, as Arnold Toynbee calls it, a *tour de force*, a tremendous effort both of thought and of action, by the holiness of her best ones and the integrity of the rest—by scholars' ink and martyrs' blood, to use a Mohammedan saying that Ernest Psichari was fond of quoting. There is nothing automatic about the help we get from God: it operates through human beings who have given themselves to God.

So though the study of the past should lead us to a profound feeling of optimism, it has to be an optimism of a very sturdy kind. At each successive stage of her earthly life the Church finds salvation by her response to human expectations, by proving her superhuman value and supernatural power by her actual deeds, by bringing salvation to people individually and to society as a whole. We must try to apply all this to our present crisis.

Human beings to-day are mad about the technical power

conferred upon them by science—excited and at the same time appalled by it. At one moment their pride in their achievements makes them quite crazy; at the next they are nearly as crazy with fear. For them to be absolute masters of their conquests they would have to be in total conformity with reason as human beings. But reason can only see things clearly when it can get to the bottom of them, get to the heart of reality, i.e., God. Without faith it can only grope and vacillate. They would also have to be absolutely free, in full control of their instincts and passions. But freedom is only really achieved when the will is orientated towards the Sovereign Good—God. And the will cannot be this without grace.

Bergson in a well-known phrase said that modern man needed a bit more soul. This bit more can only be given by the Church, because the Church is the representative upon earth of God, who strengthens reason by the gift of faith and frees freedom from its shackles by the action of his grace.

Human beings to-day are suffering from a depersonalization that has almost reached the state of dehumanization. Engulfed in great anonymous masses, often the slaves of tyrannical totalitarian states, dominated by the machine, or money, or efficiency, or all-powerful economics, they feel like things instead of people, means instead of ends, utter nonentities occasionally imagining themselves as infinities. They look for the secret of human relationships in new techniques—as though the very idea of "technique" was not absolutely opposed to any ideal of personal and social relationships. Only the Church can turn them back into persons, for she knows the secret of charity, which sees Christ in everyone, sees everyone as a single unique person with a price beyond rubies and worth an infinity of love.

Human beings to-day long for free and equal love, fully reciprocated as between man and woman. But all they find is the melancholy of mere passion, the disillusionments of the flesh, the hostility and battle of the sexes, the escape into endless dreams. Only the Church, with her teaching about the sacrament of marriage and the spiritual nature of the Christian family, can show them what true love really is— love of the self-sacrificing kind that gives itself and all it has in a fundamental equality between two different, complementary persons who are united in a joint venture throughout time and all eternity, with their children as the living embodiment of all this.

Human beings to-day are trying to find happiness. All they get is wealth and comfort, or disillusionment, or envy and rebellion. Only the Church can give them real happiness— through the living paradox of the Beatitudes, through poverty, meekness, the spirit of peace and sacrifice. Real happiness in this world and infinite happiness in the world to come.

Human society to-day wants social justice. Too often it tries to find it in a sort of mathematical equality and sacrifices freedom to it—and still, precisely because of its technology, fails to find it. It believes in the lying promises of atheistic Communism, which keep telling it that to-morrow —always to-morrow—there will be perfect justice. Only the social teaching of the Church, applied to actual conditions by human beings who have talent, initiative and courage, can give them this justice. For there can be no social justice without respect for the human person, and a generous love, a devouring charity, for human beings; there can be no social justice without a profound harmony between individuals, families, intermediate bodies and the State; there can be no social justice without a fair attitude towards work and wages and prices and a proper grading of economic activity in accordance with the human aims and objects of life in society.

Society to-day thinks it can make its members happy. If happiness means wellbeing and security the idea is not at all far-fetched, for the means are there to achieve it. But if the word is taken in its fullest sense, then such an idea seems very far-fetched indeed and almost ludicrous. The Church is there to remind society that though some of the conditions that make happiness possible are collective affairs, happiness itself remains a personal and family matter, for it is the result of freedom and is not to be imposed by law or even by such a powerfully persuasive weapon as propaganda.

Society to-day tends to be totalitarian. It likes to regard itself as absolute. The Church is there to teach it both its dignity, as the provider of the general good, and its merely relative value both in the face of the divine Absolute which is its judge, and the dignity of the human beings it is called upon to serve.

The world to-day longs for peace. Threatened by atomic wars in which the whole race runs the risk of extermination, it knows that its only chance of salvation is to be found in real peace. But though it wants peace it is unable to achieve it because it is not prepared to pay the price. The price of peace means willing and working for the other man's good. The price of peace means respect for the uniqueness and autonomy of all racial and national and cultural groups, renouncing the false dogmas of all autarkies and absolute sovereignties, all forms of nationalism and imperialism. The price of peace means accepting an external moral law above and beyond the will of any group. Only the Church can enable human beings to pay the price of peace, for she alone can give them charity, which knows no barriers or frontiers and leads to peace by basing it on justice.

The world to-day is suffering from frightful inequalities between one set of people and another and one continent and another. Half the human race goes hungry whilst privileged nations live in luxury and waste. Peace will not be established without a gradual reduction of these inequalities and the injustices they lead to. But here again we come upon the need for an immense amount of charity, and we see how essential is evangelical poverty as the condition and result of charity in the case of both individuals and groups. We discover the need for charity—and we find ourselves in the presence of the Church.

World Crisis and the Catholic

The world to-day longs for the creation of a world-wide state of culture, to be shared by all, no matter where they come from or what their background is. None of the existing cultures seems likely to lead to this, even if backed by force. It really means creating a new culture. But there can be no culture without an animating spirit behind it, without some metaphysical conception of the world and man and human life, without an absolute to support a whole scale of moral and intellectual values. Only Catholicism, with its universality, can inspire and orientate the universal culture of the future.

In the brief space of a few paragraphs I have tried to sketch both the aspirations of our age and the causes of the crisis by which it is shaken. For the very aspirations show the deficiencies, the gaps, the insolvencies. Will mankind emerge from this crisis by the *tour de force* of some provisional solution? We can hope so if we remember on the one hand the instinct of self-preservation and on the other the action of Providence. But mankind will not emerge from it if it refuses the hand offered it by the Church. And the Church will have to put all her strength into her hand and arm, if they are to pull mankind out of its blood and mire. Mankind will not find salvation without the Church. Nor will the Church achieve her own salvation or the salvation of mankind without the action of the children of God, through whom God makes his presence felt in history. That is what we learn from the past: a hope with nothing passive about it, finding its full expression in the heroic lives lived by the saints.

Gertrud von le Fort was born at Minden in Westphalia on 11th October 1876, of a noble Huguenot family which had been obliged to leave France on account of its Protestant faith. She was educated as a Protestant, studied Protestant theology in Berlin and Heidelberg, and in 1923 published the theological testament—the Glaubenslehre—*of her master, the philosopher, Ernst Troltsch. In 1924 appeared* Hymns to the Church, *and shortly afterwards, in 1925, Gertrud von le Fort was received, in Rome, into the Catholic Church.*

The Hymns *were followed by the four books which still constitute the most essential part of her complete works: 1928, the first volume of* Das Schweisstuch der Veronika *and* Römische Brunnen; *1930,* Der Papst aus dem Ghetto; *1931,* Die Letzte am Schafott, *and 1934,* Die ewige Frau. *Other important works followed, including the second volume of* The Veil of Veronica *and* Der Kranz der Engel. *An anthology has recently been published (by* Insel *and* Ehrenwirth), *while the volume,* Aufzeichungnen und Erinnerungen, *published in 1951, contains autobiographical material and critical essays which give a deeper insight into the work, and above all the personality, of Gertrud von le Fort.*

Gertrud von le Fort resides to-day at Oberstdorf in Bavaria. She is a member of the German Academy of Language and Poetry and of the Bavarian Academy of the Fine Arts. In 1947, she received the Munich Prize for Literature and in 1948, the Anette von Droste-Hülshoff Prize.

The Voice of the Church Speaks

GERTRUD VON LE FORT

Come, my children in the world, come and be my witnesses:

I need every mouth that still prays,
I need every hand that still traces the sign of the holy Cross!
For the day is heavy with storms of temptation—
There are many along the road who no more find the way
    home:
You must be light to light their way,
You must be watchers to lead them by night—
I will give priestly words into your keeping.

Come, my children in the world, and be my witnesses:
I have blessed you and you must be a blessing!